Laurie Conrad

The

SPIRITUAL
LIFE
of ANIMALS
& PLANTS

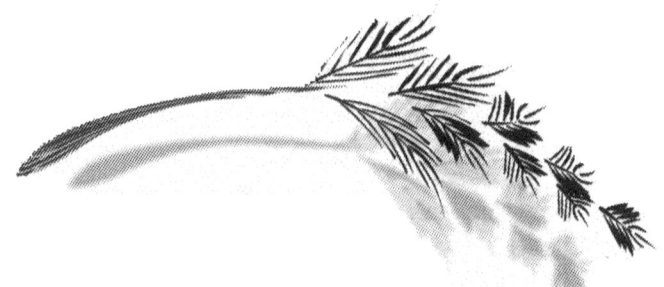

by

LAURIE CONRAD

design & ornament by

DIANA SOUZA

ISBN: 0-75965-872-2

This book is printed on acid free paper.

1st Books - rev. 1/9/02

dedicated to little Carolyn
who once heard a dying cockroach scream

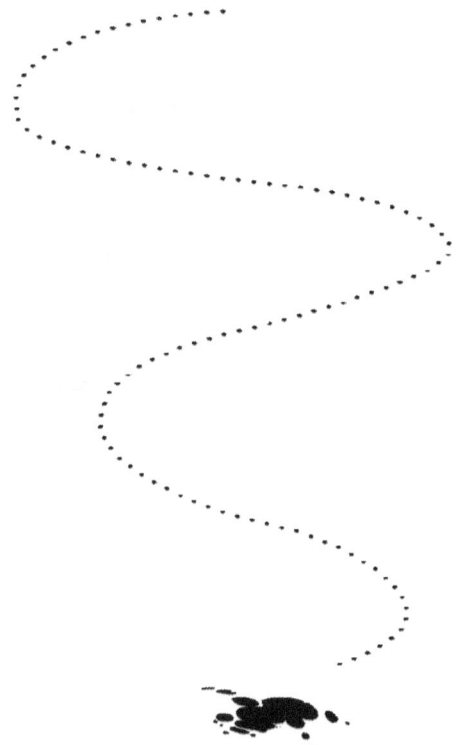

*A large percentage of the profits from this book
will be donated to organizations which
support the well being of animals*

Book Design and Illustrations by Diana Souza

(including the photo illustration of cover cat, Guy)

See more of Diana's work at

www.art-temple.com

Photos by Laurie Conrad and Diana Souza

with contributions from friends
Mariann Loveland, "Dalai Lama" page 45
Anna Maria Scholey, "Isis" page 75

*The information offered in these stories
is not intended as a substitute for medical treatment.
God works through medical doctors as well as Divine Healers!*

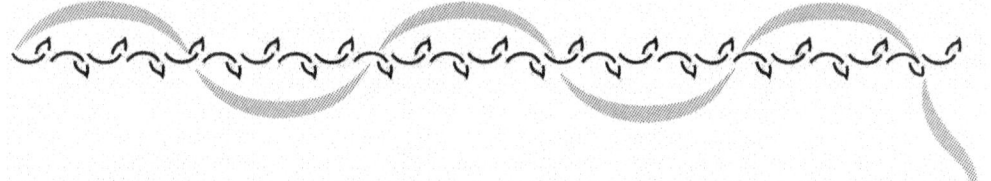

PREFACE

There are many ways to write a book. Not knowing how best to approach the topic of the spiritual lives of animals, I chose stories, not literary stories, but true accounts of the spiritual life of animals I have known.

The first stories in this volume are solely observations, for my understanding of animals was virtually nonexistent in my youth. As I observed the animals around me, however, I learned of their spiritual yearnings and innate devotion to the Divine. In this book I have tried to trace and communicate what I learned from these observations, no more no less.

My dream is that all the creatures of Earth will receive spiritual instruction, so that all can glorify God.

As I have often told the animals and trees and plants:
"People are not listening. Pray little ones, pray.
Ask mercy for yourselves and your families
and for all the beings of Earth."

STORIES

Clairvoyance

Today, in my mind, I stood
at the edge of the universe
and looked into the infinite
Wordless Wisdom alone—

Coming back
towards earth, always
awed by its colors
this gift hung by God in the night sky
about the size of my hand—
glad to call it home
from this distance
Closer, more cluttered
now the creatures of earth
the buildings and the roads
and compassion replaces awe—
I wish to fill the universe with
this compassion and bring the clarity
from the edge of the universe

But I cannot.
In the garden, so much lost—
until I look into the face
of the first spring flower.

INTRODUCTION

The concept of teaching animals to pray is not
a new one. According to first-hand accounts, birds
came from all over the world to hear St. Francis preach,
and even fish rose out of the water in order to hear St.
Anthony speak of God. The Hindu Sage Ramana Maharshi often
told his disciples that his favorite cow would reach full enlightenment. And St. Martin de Porres talked with animals, healed them,
and taught them ethics and virtues.

I was not allowed pets as a child. However, St. Francis was my
favorite saint; I often went alone to the Church, and knelt before the
statue of our gentle St. Francis in the silence of the empty church.
I don't believe I knew the legends about him then. I also didn't realize that I was clairvoyant. I often saw bright beings, but I thought
that everyone saw them.

My major encounter with an animal as a child was finding a dead
mouse, and I remember organizing and leading a cortege for him on
the way to his burial site. Never having been to a funeral, for some
reason I made placards which we carried attached to sticks. What
they said, I do not remember. I believe I carried the mouse.

1

FRED THE CAT

Fred the cat arrived when I was in my early twenties. Music was my entire life then. Late one night, standing by the old, worn stereo record player with Paderewski and Viennese Waltzes, the beauty of his interpretation – split second timings that set him apart from all the other pianists – microseconds, the left hand chords just a bit held back in places – the process of creation impressed itself on me, the mysteries of the universe unfolded in the sounds surrounding and filling me – true artists live on the rim of God, and in that moment instinctively I knew this. Music became my spirituality, and I entered on the Path of Beauty. Even though I had been raised a devout Catholic, this too was put aside during those years. Framed and unframed musical scores and photographs of composers replaced holy cards and paintings of the gentle saints.

I was in graduate school, earning a Masters in Music. The Masters in Music seemed far away from the Profundity of Beethoven, or the stirring Emotions and Power of Rachmaninoff or Chopin – studies in music, theory and form and analysis, even the composition of music itself for me had only one goal – the music itself. The rest of life was a blur, and not very real to me at that time, my world more or less started and ended each day on the piano bench. My devotion to the Piano was such that I often said I would be willing to die if I could then be but a splinter of the piano rack in my next life. In retrospect, this might explain Fred the cat's interest in music – it was the only way to get my attention.

2

Fred the cat was actually a girl. Some friends brought her, and she came with her name so I left it as it was. She seemed deeply devoted to music. I say this because Fred the cat sat on the music rack of the piano while I practiced. For hours at a stretch. Fred sat on the music rack while I practiced Czerny's School of the Virtuoso for seven hours a day for an entire hot summer. The exercises in the School of the Virtuoso repeat up to thirty-two times each, and everyone else in the house left save Fred the cat who remained stoically on the music rack.

She also appeared to be listening. I say this because for years, day after day, hour after hour, Fred always knew when the piece I was playing would end. Even a Chopin Ballade which can run over twenty minutes when practicing slowly. Consistently, three or four measures from the end of the piece she would sit up, stretch, and jump down from the piano, begging to be fed as the last notes faded into silence.

This impressed me.

THE BUMBLEBEE ON
PROSPECT STREET

I was still living with Fred the cat on Prospect Street when one of my piano students brought me some young garden plants that he had raised from seed. There they stood, Madagascar Periwinkles, all lined up in their peat pots. Since I had never had an indoor plant much less a garden, I was a bit nervous about their future.

Out front were two strips of baked, barren land perhaps seven feet long and two feet wide, interspersed with a few brave weeds and separated by a concrete walkway. As I thought wistfully of the Debussy Prelude waiting for me inside, my student surveyed the silent, cracked earth. He was pleased with the sun conditions; it was sunny, I agreed, but on further examination he found that the earth was riddled with rocks. This, he said, was a danger and undesirable – like bad notes in music– for the roots of the young plants would have to struggle for space and nutrients. In short, I would have to remove the rocks.

Trained to work hours at the piano, sometimes to perfect a few measures of music, a few notes – I approached the garden as I would a Chopin Etude. My housemate gave me a kitchen colander to use, and I sifted and dug and sifted the dry, lifeless earth again, until I was as sun scorched as the ground and only a few pebbles floated to the surface. A friend came by and said that I should leave a few rocks in the ground, for drainage. I ignored him. In fact, I unearthed so many rocks out of the twenty-eight or so square feet of property, that our landlord had to rent a truck to haul them all away.

4

In any case, I would spend hours straining a square foot of soil, several feet deep – and it was in this way that I met the Bumblebee.

The Bumblebee actually lived in a chink of the stone wall that edged our future garden. I noticed Bee not only because I was in one spot for so long mining rocks, but also because I was more or less in his flight path. Basically I was in his front yard.

After Bee had exited and entered his or her home a few times, I calmed down enough to watch him. As the hot afternoons passed, I began to notice a pattern in his behavior: he would emerge from his house and begin a small flight pattern, a small circle almost under my nose, which then increased in size and momentum, concentric circles higher and wider each time – until finally he had enough momentum to break the circular pattern and fly off into the distance. On reentry, the procedure was reversed: the circles became smaller and slower until he could easily glide to his front door. And he always wiped his feet before he entered his home.

I have often thought about this little neighbor on Prospect Street. I also have wondered if it was Bee each time, or his friends and relatives as well. Now I regret that I did not give him any prayers. He seemed like a good soul.

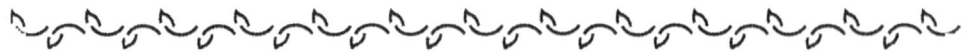

BABY BIRDS LEARN THEIR TUNES IN PHILLY

For whatever reason, I had never known a bird well. My first real imprint of bird song came one day crossing the Quarry bridge in Ithaca. It was either summer or spring, I'm not sure. However, the experience itself I will never forget. The sound. It was a flood of sound, coming from all corners of the gorge and the cliffs. Standing on the bridge, I saw not a single bird. Just sound, sound everywhere. All the birds were singing together, at the same time, but they each held to their own tune. Their own tune, at their own tempo and key. Some songs had trills, others not; there seemed to be an infinite variation of timbres and pitches and tempi, all going on at once, snatches of songs everywhere in the gorge. Being a twelve-tone composer I was fascinated. I wondered if angelic choirs would sound similar, if all the heavenly voices of all realms were heard simultaneously.

This is my only memory of birds, until I heard the baby birds learning their tunes in Philly. I was staying with a friend on the outskirts of Philadelphia one spring, for a few weeks. She was working at a stables, and for lack of other things to do, I went with her. I usually sat leaned up against a big tree to watch her, and we had our home-brought lunches there as well.

One day I noticed some music going on above me. Well, the beginnings of music. Some baby birds were learning their songs. I assumed that they were baby birds, because they seemed very inexperienced. It also appeared that some adult, undoubtedly a parent, was teaching them. This was a new concept. Birds sang. It had never occurred to me that birds had to learn their tunes.

The big tree I was leaning against had not yet fully leafed out and there were still many bare branches. One afternoon, on a bare branch, through the young leaves, I saw the mother or father bird. The only bird I have ever learned to identify by sight is a robin, and this might have been one. I'm not sure.

In any case, I was struck first by the bird's posture. Perhaps I noticed his posture because as a graduate student I was required to take voice lessons. And posture and breath support were ninety percent of my instruction. The bird's posture was everything my voice teacher wanted. His shoulders were relaxed, his back and neck in perfect position for a Carnegie Hall concert. His jaw was free. He supported from what I took to be his diaphragm, his chest expanding as it should, and his wings hung loosely at his sides. This was most intriguing, for he was so relaxed that as he sang his wings actually floated gently from his body and then back to his sides, allowing for the inhalation and exhalation of breath. Anyone who has tried to sing correctly, or watched an opera singer perform, knows what tremendous effort and body strength it requires. And the bird was working hard, that was apparent. This was another concept, that a bird would work hard at his song. The children practiced quite a lot each day, and by the time I left for Ithaca they were doing quite well, although still squeaky around the edges.

These were some of my early experiences with animals.
Except for the fly on Black Road.

THE FLY ON BLACK ROAD

Laurie, Dominique and Guinivere on Black Road

I don't have that much to say about the fly on Black Road.

Except, when he came into the music room – he actually had a presence, a personality. He had wonderful, extraordinary energy, and I've remembered him to this day, which is about fifteen years later. In any case, it was the first fly with personality that I had met.

Perhaps because of this first connection, I now seem to be able to communicate with all of them, at least in a limited way. Our conversation, besides an occasional prayer, is limited to my asking them to leave my house. I open the door – ask them to leave, and they fly out the door. Always.

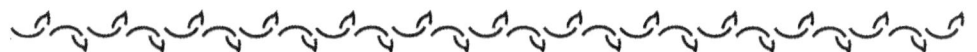

I LEARN THAT DOGS TALK

When I turned twenty-nine years old, a Russian woman taught me how to meditate. She was a scholarship piano student of mine, and after a few months of quarter and sixteenth notes and some simplified Mozart pieces she left a note for me on the piano. It said: "I no longer wish to study the piano. We will meet in metaphysics."

I didn't even know what metaphysics meant. Whatever it meant, it sounded complicated and hard, and inwardly I saw all kinds of strange scientific and alchemical symbols floating above empty sheets of paper.

Because of my Russian friend, I became interested in metaphysics and the spirituality of all religions, and wolfed down all the books on spirituality that I could find. In short, I took up the quest for enlightenment. Friends gave me photographs and paintings of various saints and sages, which I put everywhere. I scribbled Zen quotes on the walls in pencil. Interestingly enough, a painter friend drew me a scroll which said: Even a frog / can reach enlightenment / if he meditates. With a picture of a frog in the corner.

At that time I had two dogs, a black labrador named Guinivere and Dominique, who was of mixed descent. We were living on State Street, in an artists' commune, sharing space with nine other starving artists. My favorite story from this era is the man in the living room. I covered the man every night with a blanket, because he didn't have one. After some months, at one of our weekly house meetings, someone asked who the man in the living room belonged to. He didn't belong to anyone, so we asked him to leave.

The dogs and I did everything together, including meditation. We would go to the edge of one of the cliffs nearby, and meditate overlooking a waterfall. One day two birds cried and talked throughout our meditation. It sounded as though they had lost a child. When I opened my eyes, I noticed that the dogs were intently listening to every word. I say this because their ears were glued back to their heads, and the more emotional the birds became, the more flattened the dogs' bodies were against the ground. It struck me suddenly that even if the dogs couldn't understand every bird word, they certainly understood the overall content. This was a new concept. That dogs and birds might communicate.

Perhaps a month or two later Guinivere gave a very long speech from our living room to the world. This oration was in the very middle of the night, and was in response to a long series of questions or messages passed between two other dogs somewhere down the street. Guinivere stood as she spoke, and delivered an emotionally charged, and this might sound strange, noble response. She wasn't just barking back. She was inflecting a response. Her voice changed in timbre and in dynamics, in rhythm and tempo, just as a human voice would. Some sentences were soft and compassionate, others were majestic and moving. She spoke for probably ten minutes, the winter night silent and clear all around her. And she must have said it well for there was not another bark in the neighborhood after that. That the barks of a dog might have meaning, that dogs actually had a language I didn't understand – this was enlightening.

The little tan dog, Dominique, was almost a year old before her first bark. Actually, she never said anything. I attribute this to her unfortunate childhood, i.e. before she found me. The bark came about in an interesting way. Because of her various insecurities, Dominique had a little bed, well, actually a cardboard carton lined with towels that stayed close by my bed at night. This was so that I could easily

10

pat her if something came up. Towards dawn one night – well, she told me everything. Everything horrible that had ever happened to her (which seemed considerable). For about twenty minutes.

Any description would have to fall short of the original. Her voice, which was higher pitched than Guinivere's, covered an extraordinary range. She slid from the highest coloratura soprano to basso, up and down her particular scale. She would

Nell, Dominique and Guinivere

settle mid-range and give a fairly garbled account of some event, then slide back up, stay there for some instants and then back down, phrases packed with sixteenth notes and a few warbles, punctuated with what sounded like sobs. Some pitches were louder than others, some barely a whisper. Near the end of her account, there would be pauses, after which she would take another breath and add something more. It was a wrenching experience for me, the parent. The people who lived upstairs heard it as well.

Near dawn the next night, she barked for the first time in her life. It was actually more like a yodel ending in a scream. She was so embarrassed that she didn't try again for almost a year. The upstairs neighbors heard this also.

Throughout her life, Dominique had trouble expressing her feelings. In the fourteen or so years that we lived together, Dominique and I only had one other long discussion of this kind. It came about in an

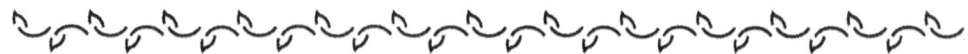

unusual way. Dominique was in the hospital recovering from a serious operation. Her veterinarian was a piano student of mine and Bobbi would stop by my house each day with a full report: Dominique looked happy and was recovering nicely. I told Bobbi that although Dominique might appear happy, she had difficulty expressing her true feelings and I had my doubts about her state of mind. "She looks fine," Bobbi-the-scientist said, and I replied, "I don't care how she looks. How does she feel?"

Bobbi agreed to smuggle me into the hospital, late at night after everyone else had left. This meant that I had to crouch in the cage with my dog, in the middle of the night, while Bobbi sat on a stool and wrote up reports on the dogs in the room. As soon as I walked in the room Dominique began her own report. It went on for about thirty minutes. After she was done I gave her a long hug and told her that she would be home soon. Bobbi locked Dominique's cage and as we left said quietly: "You were right. She had a lot to tell you." Bobbi didn't say many other words on the drive home.

It was also during this time that from readings about yogis and Catholic saints, I realized that I was clairvoyant. Clairvoyant means "clear-seeing," and can include seeing into the future, auras, the present in other locations on the earth and in other realms, and other phenomena. Until this time, I thought everyone was clairvoyant, i.e. saw what I saw. It took another half-decade or more, after wading through wads of psychic experiences, that I came to realize that "clairvoyance," at its highest, is to see through to the Divine,

to see the Divine everywhere.

THE COW ON BLACK ROAD

The house on Black Road had two barns and a silo that rose like a steeple into the sky. A true ribbon road seemed to unfurl into the distance, patterned with reflections of the sun, and nights there were very dark if there was no moon. If one walked down the rough road, you would pass cornfields and woods and fields edging the road, and the distance ahead continued and continued endlessly, harboring more fields and one couldn't quite see what else.

I lived there at some point in my early thirties, with the two dogs and Nell the cat. Cows and bulls were pastured out back in the summers, and at night their alto and basso recitatives and the sound of the frogs filled the air. There were rolling hills there, and perhaps because of the blue-green colors or the great expanse, it felt almost like living by the sea. The cows and bulls and I were separated by a series of endless white oak fences, and I actually never went to see them. I'm not sure why.

One day, as I was standing in the chamomile-covered driveway admiring an unusual sky, I looked towards the house and found myself face to face with a large bull or cow, I couldn't tell which. Frankly, whoever it was almost scared me to death (I was raised, after all, in the Bronx and on Long Island; the only animals I had seen were in the Bronx zoo). I gingerly said "hi" and then somehow, in a somewhat bowing posture, found my way to the front door. I immediately called my landlady who said if it was brown and white it was

a cow and if it was black it was a bull. The being in my front yard was brown and white, and as I looked out the window I could see her heading down Black Road towards the main road. The main road came out of a curve at Black Road, the cow would surely get hit by a car. I ran outside. She was half way to the main road. Not knowing what to do, I followed her down the road calling "Cow, here cow, here cow." No response. Then I did the stupidest thing possible – I started running to catch up with her. The cow, in turn, started running, and soon we had both turned onto the main road, cars swerving to miss us, I trying to flag down traffic. Finally one intelligent driver corralled the cow with his car, cut her off at an angle, and she ran back to her pasture, across a small copse of woods. I thanked the driver and walked back up our road, waving happily to the horses in the opposite field who had been watching.

By the time I reached my front door – there was the cow. She walked right past me and headed down the road. I said, "O no," and stood in the middle of Black Road, watching her. After some thought I said, in a firm, confident voice: "Stop." The cow stopped. She turned her

head towards me, over her shoulder. I silently but emphatically pointed to her pasture. She turned and slowly walked though the woods to her pasture. I never saw her in my yard or in the road again.

Recounting this story, I very much regret that I did not teach the cows and bulls to pray. Once I saw them herded onto trucks, from the smaller barn that stood next to my house on Black Road. They were making a terrible noise, and I went to see them. I asked some questions but now do not remember what the men said – what was their destination I wonder. I more remember being so close to the wooden ramp, amidst the noise and moving legs and hooves and eyes of the cows, perhaps I brought them peace without knowing. My heart breaks open as I now think of them, spilling onto the hills that held them. I will now send them healing and teach them how to pray in the past, for there is no past-present-future time as we think it.

Still sadness lingers. The cows and bulls and frogs and I lived so close to each other for more than two years, and I hardly knew them, or thought about them. I knew so little then.

THE HORSES AND CHOPIN

There were very few houses on Black Road, perhaps three altogether. And aside from the cows and bulls out back, the chickens and goats next door and the birds in the air and all the creatures in the fields and woods that I either saw or heard – I only met one set of human neighbors the entire time I lived in the country with the dogs and Nell the cat. Those neighbors owned the horses down the road.

My neighbors across the road had several horses. One of them, I never learned his name, would run across the field to greet me whenever I left my house – even if he was in the furthest corner of his meadow. At night, when the dogs and I and Nell the cat often walked down Black Road together, the quiet of the night would fill with soft

whinnies and neighs if I forgot to say hello or pat their noses. On reflection, I don't think I ever fed them more than a handful of grasses from the side of the road – and since their field was filled with the same grasses, no, it must have been their love for us that brought them.

The horses down the road came to the edge of their property whenever we passed them on the road, and they waited for us all in a row, lined up along their fence. My neighbors said that if they looked out their window and the horses were gone they never worried, they always knew where they were – because whenever the horses wanted to see me they would just break down the fence and come over. Often there was a horse standing in my front yard, waiting for me. After a hug or two I would walk them home, and since they wore no harness or rope we strolled side by side down the road more as friends than a person and a horse. Once home, I would tell them to stay on their property until their owners could put their fence back up. They always listened. Interestingly enough, the ground around my house was covered in hoofprints but the horses never stepped in my gardens.

In time, I began to notice their personalities. Some were shy, others very out-going, vibrant and sunny. The horse who ran across the fields to see me had a very special presence, perhaps an intelligence, or a soul quality – and I could feel it even at a great distance, even when he was in the far corner of his field. I could also feel the living connection between us – I wasn't looking for it, I just felt it, and I felt it in my heart. This all interested me, intrigued me. At the time, I remember thinking that I had not had this feeling even with a person, nor seen such soul light – somehow this horse had a greatness beyond the ordinary.

The dogs loved the horses across the road, and while Nell the cat and I greeted them from our side of the fence, the dogs would go under the fence and joyfully walk with them. Birds would sometimes sit on the backs of these horses, and I had never seen that before. The birds looked so little, perched atop the broad backs of the horses.

One day, as I practiced a Chopin Nocturne, I looked out my window and was surprised to see all the horses pressed against their fence, listening to the music. Their heads and ears were sharply pointed in my direction. I practiced for hours, mainly Chopin. And they stood at the fence listening. At least every time I looked out the window they were there. And from that point on, I always checked to see if they were there when I practiced or wrote music – and they were. Birds came and sat in the bushes by my window while I played or composed music. Groups of them, I would watch them come, from all directions, to settle on the bushes outside my window.

At one point the owners of the horses down the road asked me if I wanted to ride their horses. In fact, they asked several times. But after seeing into their hearts I could not do so. It would be like asking my best friend to carry me somewhere. No, I would meet them always on the ground, face to face and heart to heart.

BIRDS SAVE GUINIVERE'S LIFE

Birds saved my dog Guinivere's life.
For if I hadn't found her, she certainly would have died.

This is a sad story with a happy ending. I had moved to the country, in part, for Guinivere and Dominique. There was virtually no traffic on Black Road, and the dogs had all the hills and fields and forests to safely romp in. Somehow Guinivere managed to get hit by a truck on Black Road. The only truck I had ever seen go down our road.

I saw and heard the truck because it was an event in itself. About an hour later I went outside and knew that Guinivere had been hit and injured, perhaps seriously – there was much blood in the road. I called and called but she didn't come, which was also an event in itself. Guinivere always came when I called her.

I looked to the fields and the hills and the forests – and I knew that I could never find her. Not unless she came to me. She could be any-where, and the hills and fields and forests stretched to the horizons, in all directions.

Dominique and Nell the cat and I tried to find her none-the-less. I called and called, the sun sweeping the fields and the hills – but no sign of my big black dog Guinivere who would look so little in the

field, like a speck if I could find her. I was heartbroken and exhaust-
ed, for I was now sure that Guinivere was dead. Otherwise she
would have come to me, or at least answered me. Finally I just stood
where I was and asked Heaven to help me find her. I prayed for a
long time.

My meditation was broken by the sound and flurry of many little
birds. Perhaps they were the birds that sat on the backs of the horses, or the birds who sat in the bushes and listened to me play the
piano. They were clustered in one part of the vast field, actually not
too far from me, and they were very excited, chattering and flapping
their wings. I decided to investigate. And there was my Guinivere,
wounded and in shock, huddled on the floor of the field, beneath the
cluster of birds. I thanked the birds and took Guinivere into town.
She had immediate surgery, spent some days in the hospital and was
fine.

So far, I was observing animals, learning about them, learning to see
them as individuals and to understand them. I had learned to take
care of their physical and emotional needs; I had even taught them
some ethics and virtues. But I had not yet taught them to pray. I did-
n't yet know that they could.

NELL LEARNS TO PRAY

My little cat Nell. Nell appeared on my doorstep in the country, abandoned, perhaps a few weeks old. Whether she found us or was brought to us, I will never know. She was very sick with pneumonia when she arrived, and spent some weeks in the hospital getting cured. When she came home, she went everywhere with us. She took walks with us, down the road, in the woods, through the fields --and on sidewalks after we moved back into town. She loved the car, and sat on my shoulder, looking out the windows or in the mirrors. She also thought Dominique was her mother.

Nell was also a composer. She sometimes helped me to write music. I say this because often when I was thinking about what to do next, Nell would very gently jump onto the piano keys and walk on them. At first I was annoyed at this and would give her a reprimand. However, one afternoon, while working on a song cycle for piano and mezzo soprano, I got stuck. No ideas. Nell began her walk on the keyboard. She was on the octave of the piano I had last played, and was very gingerly playing beautiful notes that were in the style of the piece I was writing. Intrigued, I allowed her some freedom and she headed down the keyboard and added a few bass notes that enhanced the overall sound. Then, on her own and without any prompting from me she jumped down and went into another room. She had finished what she had to say. This happened more than once, and more than once she actually gave me ideas of what to do next.

In any case, after a year or two of living on Buffalo Street, Nell was perhaps three or four years old, I heard a very loud Clap by the rose bush. I was pruning the climbing rose at the time, and from nowhere came this loud, sharp Clap. I looked around and saw nothing. I am not usually clairaudient, but occasionally I am, so I assumed it was a sound from another realm. My thought was that something had happened to Nell.

Nell had gone for a stroll, and she did not return for three days. This absence had me very worried, not without cause as it turned out. She eventually came in her window that third evening, a broken, bloody mess.

I immediately called my student Bobbi. After a reverent examination, Bobbi said that Nell's jaw was shattered beyond repair, her skull was fractured in several places, and infection had already set in, probably during the three day absence. In all likelihood Nell would be dead by morning. We went downstairs. Bobbi said even antibiotics were useless, but that she would come the following morning and bring some in the event that Nell was still alive. Nothing could be done to save her. I thanked Bobbi, and went upstairs.

Nell was still on my futon, obviously in great pain. That she had even managed to struggle up the garden path and through the window in her condition seemed miraculous. I looked at my little grey and white cat Nell lying broken and bleeding on the bed, and my heart filled with grief and despair. Little Nell, who trusted me so, little Nell who went with us everywhere, who opened doors and loved the garden and my students and her spot by the window was now in such pain and dying...... Bobbi would have done anything in the world

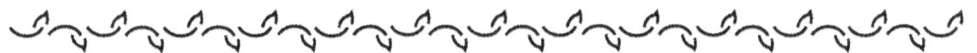

to save her, I knew that. Bobbi who had taken Polaroid photos of Dominique in the hospital, so that I could have proof that my little tan dog was doing well and was taken care of during those weeks away from me, Bobbi said Nell was dying and nothing could be done. My heart was breaking.

I don't know why, but I sat down on the floor next to Nell who was on the futon, looked her in the eye and said: "I'm going to teach you to pray. I'm going to teach you the Ave Maria, which is a prayer to the Madonna, and we are going to say the prayer all night until you are well." And we did. I said it quietly out loud, and we prayed until I literally fell asleep saying it, which was sometime after dawn. I woke up around eight or nine A.M., still on the floor with my head on the futon and Bobbi standing over me. "Where's Nell?" she asked, "I brought the antibiotics." I said, "I don't know" because I didn't. We ran downstairs, which was basically the living room and kitchen – and there was Nell eating crunchies from her breakfast bowl. With great relish. Nell bounded happily towards us, begging for milk and wet food, which I gave her, and then demonstrated her return to perfect health by asking to go outside. Bobbi-the-scientist was in total shock. I was ecstatic. Bobbi examined her thoroughly, looked up at me and said, "I don't believe this. This cat is entirely healed. What did you do?" "We prayed," I said. "All night." Bobbi had nothing to say, the evidence was standing right by her feet, brushing against her legs. Being a scientist, she couldn't call it a miracle. She just stood there, staring down at Nell. Finally she handed me the plastic vial of antibiotics. "Here," she said. "It seems like you don't need these, but keep them just in case." Of course, we never needed them. It was a miracle. The first one that I had noticed.

GUINIVERE AND BEETHOVEN

My dog Guinivere slept or dozed through up to eleven hours a day of my playing the piano, as well as several hours a day of students. I never really wondered if she enjoyed music or not, or whether she even listened, until a student began work on Beethoven's Waldstein Sonata, the last movement.

Guinivere had never heard the Waldstein, neither on recording nor in person – I had never studied it. One Saturday morning, one of my protegés came in and played the last movement for me, almost up to tempo and with much feeling. At some point, I noticed that Guinivere was sitting up instead of lying down. Then I noticed that she was facing the piano, and seemed to be listening intently. In fact, she was totally absorbed in the music, her body completely alert, head erect, ears up and back. She sat there, motionless for quite some time... until she realized that I was watching her. Once she was aware of my gaze, she pretended that nothing was happening, and very slowly, nonchalantly stretched out on the rug in her usual eyes closed position. Pretending to be asleep.

I mentioned this to my student, and thought nothing more about it. I love Beethoven, why shouldn't a Labrador Retriever?

The following year some new neighbors moved in next-door. They had a powerful, fine stereo system, and on some hot summer days they took it onto their porch. One day, late summer, I looked out

my kitchen window into the garden and there was Guinivere, in the corner of the garden nearest our neighbor's porch. That itself was unusual. What was more unusual was that she was sitting up, facing their porch and obviously listening intently to their stereo; I had never seen her do that before. Her attention was entirely fixed on the music, in fact when I went into the garden she didn't even notice me. I stood there for some time; Guinivere didn't move until the piece ended. It was Beethoven's "Emperor Concerto," his fifth piano concerto, a piece that Guinivere had heard many times. I was puzzled, so I asked my neighbors what recording they had just played. They said "The Emperor Concerto by Beethoven." I said, "Who was the pianist?" They said, "Claudio Arrau." The mystery was solved. Guinivere was used to Artur Rubinstein.

Of course, I have many more stories of Guinivere and music. However, I thought I might share someone else's story about Guinivere. My friend Eleanor once took Guinivere on a car trip. She and Guinivere were in the backseat, the driver and his wife in the front seat. The car had a beautiful stereo system, and a classical tape was playing opera full volume. At one point the friend's wife turned to Eleanor and said, "You know, it almost looks as though that dog is listening to the music." Eleanor replied, "She is listening to the music. She's used to the very best."

GUINIVERE MEETS A SAINT

In my experience, all animals are psychic, if not clairvoyant. At least the ones I have met. I say this for several reasons. Firstly they can hear what I am saying inwardly, that is they respond to what I say inwardly. Secondly, I have seen them respond to words and events in other realms. Perhaps I should explain.

I, being clairvoyant, see into other realms. This includes seeing people or beings who are no longer "alive," or better stated, are no longer in the body. And when I see a being from another realm sitting in the rocking chair, so do all the animals in the room. I say this because no matter what else is going on in the room, if I see someone in the rocker I then notice that all my pets have been looking at the rocker also. Sometimes I notice all my pets are looking at the rocker, and then I will see that someone is seated there.

The same with clairaudience. When I was in my twenties, I heard the sweetest voice imaginable softly calling my name. I was walking with Guinivere and Dominique and Nell the cat, and we were on the corner near the Catholic Church, on Seneca Street. I looked up at the statue of Mary which stands on the outside of the Church, and wondered if She had called my name. Then I said to myself, "This is very, very strange, don't think about it, just go home." Which I did. However, when almost at the end of the next block I noticed that Guinivere wasn't with us. I called her name several times, and then spotted her on the corner near the Catholic Church. She was still standing there, and she was looking in all directions, as though trying to locate the beautiful, sweet voice.

At the time I was not impressed by Guinivere's psychic abilities, I was just grateful that she had them. Guinivere was the most sane creature I had ever met, and if she heard the voice then the voice existed.

Guinivere was about eight years old when she developed a lump on the left side of her face. I could see that she was in pain, and every once in a while she would sit up and give a yelp. Nor would she let me go near the lump, instead she turned her face away from me whenever I approached her. It was very late at night, and I didn't know what to do. I finally asked that a saint come and look at Guinivere and give her whatever healing she needed to get her through the night. The saint came. Immediately. I say this because I saw him. Guinivere saw him also. He walked over to her, and she lifted her face towards him and showed him the lump. He stood over her for some time and then left. Guinivere laid down and peacefully went to sleep. The next day I took her to the veterinarian. It was an infected tooth, and they pulled it.

Since that night I never hesitate to call on a saint.
And in my experience – they always come.

27

GUINIVERE AND OUR LORD

Guinivere, the big black dog with the big floppy ears was my first dog; she was intelligent, playful, and had a heart that could fill a city block. Guinivere, who was also probably one of the healthiest dogs that ever lived, died at age ten from leukemia within weeks. It was one of the greatest shocks of my entire life. It also brought me to Divine Love.

In my garden, along the rock path to my house, stood a stone statue of Christ. A statue of the Sacred Heart. Guinivere, to my knowledge, had never paid any special attention to it. We also had a picture of Christ, framed, on the living room floor. It leaned against one of the legs of the piano, and I had put it there for my little piano students. In group lessons they often sat on the floor in front of it while working on their notes or listening to another student play technique or pieces.

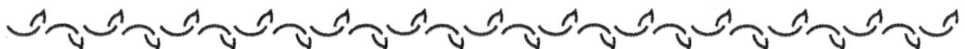

Yogananda mentioned in his **Autobiography of a Yogi** that paintings and photographs of saints and Divine Beings emit an energy that has been scientifically measured in Indian laboratories. Therefore, whether my little beginning students looked at the painting or not, they might at least soak up its beneficial rays. If nothing else, I could look at it during lessons.

As Guinivere became more ill, I noticed that she slept closer and closer to this painting of Christ, until her head was actually resting against it. By this time she was already blind from the leukemia. Soon after she began sleeping outside at night to be near Christ's statue. She lay before His statue day and night, her head at His feet resting on the flowers. Guinivere, who had never left my side now chose the bigger Light, that of Christ. It was early fall, and to be near her often Dominique and I slept in the garden as well.

One night it began to rain, and I went out onto the porch to call her inside. She wouldn't come. I called again. No response. I could see her lying in the garden, her head by Christ's feet. It was beginning to pour, and finally, in desperation, I said, "Guinivere, I don't want you to get sick. It's raining, you shouldn't get wet, you'll get a chill." No response. After a little thought I said, "Guinivere, have you forgotten, there's a picture of Christ in the living room." Before the words had echoed into silence Guinivere was on her feet. She was extremely ill, she was blind, she was very weak. But she jumped to her feet, climbed the porch step, went in the front door directly to the painting of Christ and lay down before it. She put her nose on it and went to sleep. She didn't even lick my hand as she passed me on the porch.

This is the truth, and the whole truth. Moreover, at the time – I'm not sure that I would have believed this story if I had not seen it myself.

29

MIRACLES AND GUINIVERE

By this time, I had studied Divine healing with my teacher John
Payne. During the first, and actually my last lesson on "laying-on-
of-hands" type healing, I healed him. At first I took on his pain, my
arms actually hurt. He said, "You are doing it wrong. Ask that you
be a channel of the Divine Healing Energy. Let It come through you."
Then he said a sentence I will never forget. He said, "The Divine
Energy is all around us," and I saw it. I literally saw it.

After I became proficient in this, he taught me "mental healing,"
again in one or two lessons, and over the phone. In this healing one
does not have to put hands on another, or even be in the same room.
Or even the same country. The "healer" just asks for the healing and
says "thank you" to God. It is actually a deep prayer, from the Heart.
Guinivere was one of the first recipients of my training, as well as
some violins and violas and cellos in Washington D.C., which I glued
back together over the phone for a violin maker. Over the years people began asking for healing as well. I have seen so many "miracles"
by now that they are no longer miraculous. Rather they merely
reflect the Higher Laws of a Higher Reality.

In all healing, the healer must first ask permission from the Higher.
As John said : "We are not always allowed to send healing. There is
a Divine Plan. If we are not allowed to send healing it is because the
person is in Higher Hands." And Guinivere was meant to leave Earth,
I couldn't change that. But we were allowed some things. For
example, the physicians would test Guinivere for some side issue

or problem and the test would come back positive; I would ask for healing and a few days later, on the re-test, the results would be negative. This happened often, and the veterinarian looked so puzzled and confused, especially when Guinivere's eyesight partially returned, that in the end I had to tell her that I was a healer.

She took it fairly well. I offered to help her in her work, and told her that she could call on me as needed in extreme cases. She replied that she was a scientist, working in a scientific framework, a scientist hired and paid by Cornell University, and therefore she could not accept my offer. Since then I periodically send Christ and St. Francis to all the animals in all hospitals, for comfort, instruction and healing, and help transitioning to other realms if needed.

In addition to the smaller "miracles," and there were many, there was one large one that the veterinarian at Cornell never knew about. It happened in my living room.

Guinivere was too weak to stand. This was the one thing I had dreaded. The memory is so clear, as though I were standing there now, in my living room on Buffalo Street. Too distraught to follow any given healing method, I just stood in my living room and cried: "God, please God, if she can't walk I'll have to put her to sleep, I can't carry her, she's too heavy for me." My entire Heart was in that prayer, which I suspect made up for the lack of protocol. In any case, the room began to fill with an enormous, incredible Love, what I now would call Divine Love. I could even see it, crystalline and clear, filling the room, as tangible as heat coming up the heat vents in winter. I looked down at Guinivere, and actually saw the poison receding from her legs, I watched the swelling disappear inch by inch. It took less than a minute. Guinivere stood up, wagged her tail vigorously and then gave my hand a lick. She walked until the very end of her

31

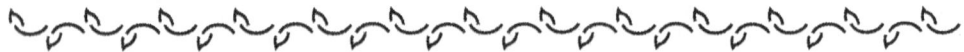

life. During this reprieve, we had some nice moments together. That Saturday afternoon we listened to a Met broadcast of Sampson and Delilah over the radio. I let Guinivere listen with headphones, not too loud and not directly on her ears. She was grateful, and we all cried. Within days she had deteriorated terribly, she barely knew me, and then for only a minute at a time. The evening before the vet came to put my Guinivere to sleep I asked one of my students to play a beautiful Bach aria, and Guinivere and I listened together, my arm around her neck. That night I played "Sheep May Safely Graze" until I more or less fell asleep at the piano. When the vet came, Guinivere was lying by Christ's statue in the garden, and I held her and put my hand on her heart as the shot was given. She was gone in seconds. And as she left the body, the brightest Being I had ever seen stood before us. In fact the Being was so Bright that I couldn't even look at it. Whether it was Guinivere's soul, or a being that had come for her, or both, I don't know. There was too much Light for me even to make out a form. I wouldn't be at all surprised if it was Christ Himself, Guinivere was so devoted to Him.

BIRDS I HAVE KNOWN

Aside from the birds I heard from Quarry Bridge, and the birds learning their tunes in Philly, and the birds on Black Road, I really didn't know too many birds well. The little, frail old lady who lived next door said birds came every day to swim in the birdbath I had put in the garden, but I never saw them.

However, birds, as in the country, would flock to my window when I practiced – although, in town, only at dawn. And they would sing and chirp as I played, a joyful chorus outside my window. They would sing at dawn outside the window by the piano even if I had gone to bed early, as though they knew I was a fellow musician and would enjoy the concert.

Even so, I knew no birds truly personally until Nigel began practicing his song outside my bedroom window.

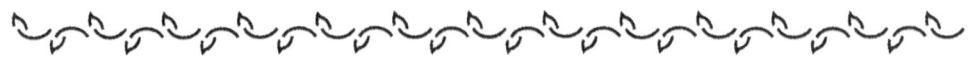

NIGEL PRACTICES HIS ARIA

The interesting thing about Nigel practicing his song, was that he always practiced it outside my bedroom window, and he always waited until I went to bed. No matter when I went to bed.

The house on Buffalo Street was really a little converted carriage house, and one bedroom wall was entirely a window. There was a beautiful old oak just outside the window, and Nigel would sing from there.

At first I thought little about his singing, except that I enjoyed it, he had such a sweet tone. Then I began to observe that he came night after night, and always began just after I had turned out my bedroom light. This led me to believe that he was not just singing, he was singing to me.

Because of this, I began to listen more carefully.

The first thing I noticed was that his song – even for a concert pianist with a tremendous technique – was very difficult. His aria contained many trills, mordents and also a huge leap to an extremely high note which was perhaps the equivalent of a high D above the staff for a human soprano. A taxing program! After a week or so, I began to realize that he was practicing. And lying there night after night, about to drift off to sleep, with no other sound in the universe but Nigel's lone aria – I began to give him instruction inwardly. I had been, after all, a piano teacher for over twenty years.

More accurately, I began evaluating his singing, and telling myself what might help him. His sound for instance – a sweet tone, but a bit fuzzy around the edges. The trills and mordents were good, but still a bit sloppy, his articulation could stand some improvement etc. Interestingly enough, it seemed that my private, unspoken criticisms seemed to guide his practice.

If I inwardly commented on his sound, his sound improved. If I thought his articulation a bit off, he began to work on articulation. And so on. Most fascinating to me, he practiced his song in sections, a phrase or less at a time. Which is how all musicians practice. Some nights he left all the trills out, other nights he practiced them separately. Other nights he would try the song with the trills, and if he made a mistake, he would go back to the beginning and try again. At the end of some weeks his sound was rich and centered, articulation and trills and mordents, his rhythm and phrasing were excellent – and I inwardly told him so. However, the leap, the big leap to the high note was still imperfect. He was still often cracking or missing the high note altogether, even though he practiced it religiously.

On the whole, I was struck not only by his musicianship, his talent – but also by his perseverance and, well, respect for his song. He obviously was striving for perfection, but in addition he always sang his

35

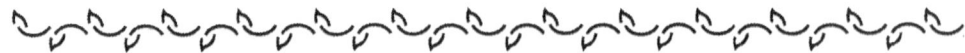

song full out, as though giving a concert before God or in Carnegie Hall, which is how I practice. I never just "run through the music," as many human musicians do. And neither did he, although as a vocalist he did sometimes practice sections at a lower volume in order to save his voice. Which I respected. He sang for me as though I were his Teacher, and with every ounce of awareness and strength he had. I thanked him for that, and hold great admiration for him, even to this day so many years later.

Then Nigel stopped coming. Perhaps for weeks. I missed him and his sweet song and devotion, and wondered what had become of him. Then one night, just after turning out the lights – there he was. He sang – so sweetly – his tone even better than before, his pitches perfect, the trills and mordents impeccable, phrasing, everything had improved. I awaited the big leap with anticipation – it was perfect. A perfect attack, on pitch, a beautiful round full sound – it was Maria Callas at her best. Inwardly I applauded him, and thanked him for singing his aria for me. He sang it just that one time that night, and I never heard him sing again.

I have thought about him often. Perhaps in those weeks away he had gone off to practice on his own. Or perhaps he had decided that it was time to study with someone else. He might have returned that last night to show me what he had accomplished in his absence, or to express his gratitude.

These things I will never know.

BERTRAM THE BIRD
ON STATEN ISLAND

Shortly after Nigel's final performance in Ithaca, I went to visit some friends on Staten Island. And from far down the street, just before dawn, I heard Bertram the bird trying Nigel's virtuoso song. His tone was thin and sickly, his mordents and trills were mere slurs, Bertram had absolutely no sense of rhythm or phrasing – in short, he and the tune were a mess. He too practiced every night, but with no visible improvement, poor thing – he had no musical aptitude, and for a bird it must have been humiliating.

After a week or so I inwardly told Bertram that the song was very difficult, that it would take much practice, and that I couldn't go through it with him, I didn't have the patience. I never heard him again, and I assume that he must have found another teacher.

THE DOG ON STATEN ISLAND

Several times a year I would stay with friends on Staten Island, some-times for weeks at a stretch. They lived in St. George, which is near the ferry. And on the way from the ferry to their house I passed a gro-cery store guarded by a large tan brutish dog on a chain – whose aura, by the way, was terrible.

The dog was chained outside the store in all weather, and the owner mentioned that at night the dog was locked in the basement. Not a great life for a dog, or any other being for that matter. The dog growled if you came anywhere near him, and was in general other-wise non-responsive and churlish. In time, as I learned about the spiritual yearnings and the spiritual development of animals, I decid-ed that this dog needed spiritual training – for the sake of his own soul, but also for the souls of those around him, including his mas-ter. Following a low, short growl from my student-to-be, I stood before him and inwardly told him of Jesus and Mary and the saints. I told him that if he were a good doggie, one day he would go to a beautiful realm filled with love, where there were gardens and beau-tiful, kind, people and saints and dog biscuits and everything else he could ever want – and I sent him a mental image of such a place, bathed in Sunshine and Peace. He pretended that he was annoyed and not listening, but I could see that he was listening, and he was even thinking. I mentally asked St. Francis to come and speak with the dog, and to watch over him in general. I told the dog to pray everyday: i.e. to tell Christ and Mary that he loved them and that he wanted to be a good doggie. Since the grocery store was only a block away, and on the main street, I saw him many times that visit. I

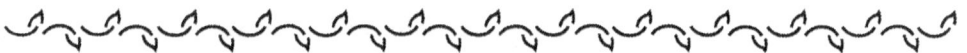

repeated my lecture every time I saw him, and his aura did seem somewhat improved by the time I left Staten Island.

I returned to Staten Island a few months after. I had actually forgotten about the unhappy guard dog, but as I turned the corner to the main street – the dog was waiting for me, his head turned in my direction, as though he knew I was coming. Even though he was chained in front of the grocery store halfway down the block, I saw him instantly. I saw him instantly because his aura was so filled with Light that he shone. Out of all the people and strollers and stores and buses and cars and a plethora of other perceptions – my attention was riveted on the dog's Light.

The dog began to pray as I walked towards him, and I say this because of his posture and also because his aura brightened further.

To see such a change in a being, in such a short time, was remarkable, and I told him so. He acted a bit shy with me – although he still maintained his guard dog persona, which was appropriate. In short, he was a changed dog. I saw him almost every day of my visit, and encouraged him to continue his practices when I left Staten Island.

A few months later, back in Ithaca, late one night (and I'm embarrassed to say that I was watching Star Trek on television), suddenly, as sometimes happens, a little movie started playing in my head. I closed my eyes to better see, and there were dogs, hundreds of dogs, all sizes and shapes, colors and breeds, sitting in a single line, one behind the other, it seemed for miles – as far as one could see to the horizon. They were all well behaved, and seemed happy and expectant, a little excited, yet sitting quietly in that long, very long, orderly row. Then, as though the camera taping the show zoomed in for a

close-up, suddenly I was standing over the tan dog from Staten Island. There was no mistake about it, it was him. Wonderingly, I turned in the other direction, to see where all these dogs were facing, where the line began. There were only a few dogs ahead of the dog from Staten Island – and at the head of the line stood Christ. Other dogs were playing and running in a beautiful countryside nearby. Then the inner movie dissolved.

I didn't know what the clairvoyant movie meant.

Six months or so later I returned to my friends on Staten Island. As I came to the corner I expected the Staten Island dog to turn his head my way, and greet me with his prayers as he had done on my last visit. He did not, in fact he wasn't there. I went inside the cluttered grocery and found the owner. "Where's your doggie?" I asked. Of course, no one in the world, I'm sure, had ever called his guard dog a doggie before. He looked a little puzzled and then offhandedly said "Oh, the dog – he died about six months ago," and then he turned and talked loudly with a customer.

About six months ago was when I had watched the clairvoyant vision. And even as I write this, so many years later, I am filled with such love for the dog on Staten Island who accomplished so much so quickly – a poor guard dog who freed himself from his difficult life and gained a beautiful realm where Christ Himself would come.

DOMINIQUE AND THE MANGER

Dominique was a delicate angel. She was deeply sensitive, and very shy. She was also sickly her entire life and rarely left her little L.L. Bean bed except to take walks with Guinivere and me. Because of her frayed nervous system, her attention span was fairly limited and she was mainly a bunch of nerves.

She loved Guinivere and also cats. She loved Guinivere to the extent that if I filled both their food dishes with dinner and Guinivere wasn't around to eat, Dominique wouldn't touch Guinivere's food. She quietly finished what was in her bowl and then returned to her plaid L.L. Bean bed. That was true love. She had respect for all beings. In the garden, along the walk, if a pansy or petunia had drooped onto the walk she would first put her nose to it in a gentle greeting and then gingerly step around it. As though it were a person, or another dog or cat.

And cats not only adored her, they brought her their kittens to take care of. As soon as the kittens could open their eyes to light, they were placed on the L.L. Bean bed with Dominique. This began with Nell on Black Road, and continued until the end of Dominique's life. Figaro,

Sergei

41

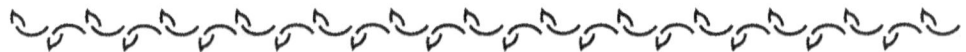

Alice's son, grew up thinking Dominique was his mother, as did every other cat I ever owned while Dominique was alive. When Angela and Alice had twelve kittens between them Dominique could barely fit on her bed.

One night, on our evening walk, I saw a small crowd of people clumped around something across the street, in front of the Catholic Church. I decided to investigate, and of course the dogs came with me. Nell was instructed to wait on the corner because she was not allowed to cross streets. She always waited. At the time this seemed perfectly natural, although now it seems astonishing.

It was a creche, a manger scene, for Christmas. It was up on a wooden table, and was magical. Real hay and a rough manger and wonderful porcelain figures of Mary and Joseph and the Infant in his cradle, the shepherds, and the animals grouped around the Infant Jesus. For some reason I thought Dominique would enjoy seeing the creche, so I lifted her up creche height. Her reaction was noteworthy. For the first time that I knew of, in her harassed and frightened life, she went completely limp. In fact she was just hanging from my arms. Oblivious to the commotion around her, that in itself a small miracle, her eyes were riveted to the figures of the Infant Christ, Mary and Joseph. She barely breathed. She was not a heavy dog, but we stood there for so long I finally had to put her down.

Who knows what my little dog Dominique saw and felt as she gazed at the Manger scene. Or Guinivere by Christ's statue. Watching them, the only thing that mattered to me was that I and others take care of not just the physical and psychological and ethical – but also the spiritual training of these souls in our care.

42

DOMINIQUE AND THE DUCK

Dominique

Dominique hated water. Absolutely. Guinivere, on the other hand, loved water and could swim indefinitely, usually with a stick in her mouth.

After years of encouragement, Guinivere and I had gotten Dominique to the point where she would at least run into the lake at Stewart Park, at least up to her knees. On a hot day.

A grand victory. One hot summer afternoon Louise and I and her little girl Carolyn decided to go to Stewart Park. I opened the car door and both Guinivere and Dominique raced towards the lake. I watched Dominique with pride. She was acting like a dog at last.

Guinivere stopped briefly on shore to choose a nice rock, Dominique passed her and ran towards some ducks enjoying the lake. She had learned this from Guinivere. The ducks began to move slowly forward, Dominique running joyfully behind them. Suddenly the last duck turned and faced Dominique. The duck delivered a loud and emotional reprimand which, if not completely understood by everyone watching from shore – well, the essence of the duck's message was clear. Dominique stopped in her tracks, slowly turned around and headed for shore. Actually she headed towards me. My heart sank. It was a hard thing for a parent to watch. As she approached I said, "Dominique, the duck doesn't own the lake, go back in and play, it's a beautiful day." Dominique sat in my lap and wouldn't budge. For the rest of the afternoon.

Guinivere meanwhile had found the perfect rock to hold in her mouth, and as usual had joined the ducks in formation, in the last row. They were now almost in the middle of the lake, just dots surrounded by swatches of sun.

I heard some voices from behind us. One said, "I say, what is that there out in the middle of the lake?" They were British tourists of some sort, and one was holding binoculars. The other said, "They appear to be ducks." The first one said, "No, with the ducks. It looks like a seal." Little Carolyn turned around and said, "That's Guinivere." Dominique gave a short sigh.

DOMINIQUE MEETS
HIS HOLINESS THE DALAI LAMA

The Dalai Lama of Tibet with Anthony Damiani at Wisdom's Goldenrod*

Dominique met the Dalai Lama of Tibet on His Holiness' first visit to the United States. The world has since found out that he is a great spiritual being, a great spiritual leader. He is, in fact, the Incarnation of Compassion and carries great Light and Power. Dominique was one of the first Americans to see this.

The Dalai Lama, on his first tour of our country, gave a lecture in Syracuse, and also spoke to us at Wisdom's Goldenrod, a philosophic Center in Valois, New York. His departure at the small Ithaca air-

---

*Anthony Damiani was my philosophy and meditation Teacher at Wisdom's Goldenrod. A selection of his writings are available through Larson Publications, New York.

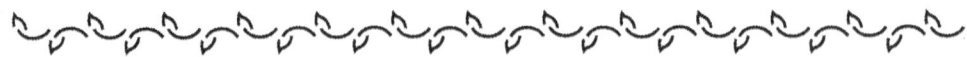

port was not announced in the newspapers; in fact his visit was not made public for various security reasons. Therefore, only members of Wisdom's Goldenrod were there that morning. Since it was a work day, perhaps only one hundred people or so turned up, huddled together in clumps against the chill. I brought Guinivere and Dominique so that they could meet such a great spiritual man. I was a little concerned about bringing Dominique, not only because of the commotion, but also because she had never been to an airport, nor seen a plane. In the end I brought her.

The Dalai Lama finally appeared, bowing and smiling to us, and he slowly made his way through the deferential offshoots of the crowd of people who tried to catch his smile or in some way show their gratitude for all that he gave and represented.

Inwardly I said, "I will never forget you" and I was fairly overcome with emotion. His Love and his Light were so very strong, it was a tangible Presence. This man, the spiritual and political head of Tibet, now in exile, had begun his spiritual training as the Dalai Lama at the age of four and had devoted his entire life to meditation and prayer. And not for himself or only Buddhists, his people – but for the world.

I was towards the back of the crowd, craning to see him board his chartered plane. The ramp was in place, the engines had started, creating a huge wind as well as a rush of noise. I tearfully watched this great man, the Dalai Lama of Lost Horizons, board the ramp with his monks and security guards and Dominique. DOMINIQUE. My little dog Dominique whose teeth literally chattered if a stranger said hello to her, Dominique who was chased out of the lake by a duck was fol-

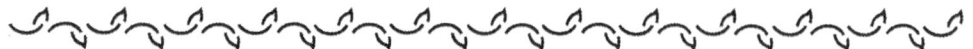

lowing the Dalai Lama up the ramp into the plane. At which point I ran to the wire fence (there's a photograph of one hundred serene people saying goodbye to the Dalai Lama at the airport and then one very unhappy, frantic person at the fence, yelling something to someone not in the photograph) and started calling Dominique's name through the din of the plane and the inner mantras of the crowd.

Dominique, who in the distance seemed to be actually wagging her tail, was boarding a plane with its engines running, with a group of strangers, and without me, the only person she had ever trusted in her uncertain short life save the cats and her L.L. Bean bed. I began screaming her name, and finally the monks kindly, but firmly chased her in my direction. Otherwise my little dog would have finished out her life in Dharmsala, India where the Dalai Lama now resides.

This story, perhaps better than any other, illustrates the spiritual yearnings and devotion of animals. They seem, in fact, to be more aware of spiritual, holy, sacred energy than the average human being. In part perhaps because of their clairvoyance, their sensitivity, perhaps from their innate need for devotion and loyalty. True, Dominique already had much spiritual training. Perhaps the average dog would not have followed the Dalai Lama up the ramp. Guinivere stayed by my side, but as we have seen, Guinivere was devoted to Christ, Christ was her spiritual Master. Perhaps Dominique was a Buddhist. This actually would not surprise me. If one were to examine her features – she did look a bit Chinese. She did not lie by Christ's statue, nor His picture in the living room. Although she was transfixed by the creche. I had not yet looked for these things, I myself was yet a beginner in the spiritual lives of animals.

DOMINIQUE'S MIRACLES

Dominique and Saints

I have found that animals, on the whole, are more open to mental, or Divine Healing than the average human. Perhaps in part because they have more trust and faith in what humans tell them. Perhaps they are more open to Divine Love. Perhaps they are emotionally less complicated. I don't know.

Dominique, being constantly in the midst of some ailment or accident, was a good being to practice healing on. There were many miracles, too numerous to relate. To illustrate what mental or Divine Healing can do: most people think that because you are sending mental healing, the medicine you send is mental: Yes and no.

Everything is mental. In that sense, yes. Is the medicine you send just a mental image of medicine? No. It is the "real" medicine, the physical medicine.

I am saying "mental healing" only to distinguish it from "laying on of hands" type healing, where the patient is physically touched by the "healer." Both are forms of Divine Healing, i.e. the healing is given directly, and purely, by God. My teacher John Payne used to call Him "The People Upstairs." You can call Him who you wish, it is still the One God who gives Life and maintains it.

Also, for the sake of convenience I am saying that I send healing. No, I am asking that healing be given, and from God. It is a prayer, a short prayer. God sends the healing, not I or any other healer. In fact, the greater the healer, the more he or she knows that he or she is nothing, not even a channel, and the greater the miracles.

For instance: one day, walking the dogs, I saw that Dominique's eyes looked terrible and that she looked miserable. She needed eye drops each day because her eyes did not produce tears (this might have been symbolic of her inability to express her feelings). I had forgotten to give her the medicine that day, she was suffering, we were out on the street on an errand and headed away from home – so I asked that she be given her eye medicine. Usually I am not allowed to do this – if the medicine or cure is easily available, I am not supposed to bother Heaven with a superfluous request. However, this day, perhaps because I felt so much love for Dominique in that instant, and felt badly because it was my forgetfulness that was causing this innocent little dog pain, because the medicine was at home on the kitchen table

and we were walking downtown – it was allowed. And her eyes filled with the medicine. Anyone, clairvoyant or not, would have seen Dominique's eyes fill to the brim with the tears.

You might say I have seen several miracles at least, per day for the last fifteen or twenty years – it's now almost a continual miracle. Even so, each time I am filled with such gratitude and such Love for the Divine. Imagine – a scrawny little tan dog standing on Cayuga Street in Ithaca, New York on a grey late fall day, the sun very small and pale in the sky beyond the church steeple, a few stray leaves left over from October milling around here and there, standing next to a big, black Labrador retriever who was a bit overweight and had very big ears, and me, in an old worn jacket with half its buttons missing and sneakers instead of boots, a poor musician waiting for traffic to stop so that I could cross and get a small worthless errand done and be back in time for my first piano student, who probably had forgotten their book and hadn't practiced anyway ...these were the beings our Shining, Radiant, Good God in Heaven, surrounded by angelic realms and beings – conferred Grace on, in the form of perfect eye drops that filled the scrawny, frightened, silly looking doggie's eyes better and more fully than the best nurse could ever do. I looked at Dominique's eyes, filled to the brim with the sacred tears, and thanked God for His

L o v e.

Perhaps a more striking example of mental healing with Dominique was the day her eyesight was restored. This was near the end of her fragile life. She had been almost completely blind for many years, but one day, unnoticed by me, she went completely blind.

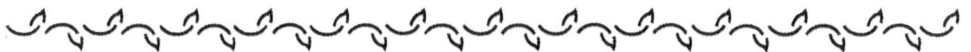

She was also deaf at the end of her life. I think that I did not notice her deafness immediately because our inner dialogue was so strong. I would inwardly say "Let's take a walk" and she would be standing by the front door. I left the deafness alone because she seemed much calmer when she was deaf. Except for the Dalai Lama's plane years earlier, noise had always frightened her.

However when it became apparent that she had become completely blind, and that she was miserable and frightened because of it, I asked that her sight return, at least in part. It did, and within minutes. She was given partial sight, and could see well enough for comfort until she died.

Zoya, who was staying with me at the time said, "I'm so glad Dominique can see again. She wasn't happy blind," and ran out the door to go to school. Zoya was used to miracles by then. And that is how it should be, for everyone. Divinity is everywhere, always. We have only forgotten – we have forgotten our own Divine Nature, and we have forgotten what I call God.

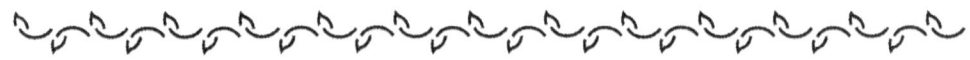

THE CATS MEET ST. FRANCIS
IN THE GARDEN

St. Francis came in the mail. He was a foot and a half high, made of some grey stone or concrete – he had a small bird in his hand and a slender deer by his side. I loved him instantly.

Three generations of cats lived with me then: Angela, her daughter Alice, and Alice's son Figaro. They rarely got along. In fact, they did very little together except to eat their meals in the same room and watch television together, and that only occasionally.

I already knew where St. Francis would stand in the garden. There was an arched vault carved into the mock orange shrub in one corner of the garden, he would fit there nicely. It was a sort of natural chapel, and seemed appropriate for a saint who loved the outdoors and Nature.

Two friends, Cathy and Eleanor came up the path, and I introduced them to small St. Francis, who humbly stood by his box on the kitchen table. It was a splendid summer day, birds and bugs were singing, and after some discussion about the life of St. Francis, it was decided that he should immediately go into the garden. I walked the stone path to the chosen spot in the garden carrying the statue – and suddenly I realized that all three cats were behind me on the path, walking single file and fairly evenly spaced on the path. That was, in itself very unusual. When St. Francis was installed by the dahlias and under the arched boughs of the mock oranges, I stood back to survey the scene. As I did so, Angela and her daughter Alice, and Alice's son Figaro stepped forward and formed a perfect semicircle before the statue and then sat down, facing the statue. They remained seated there for quite a while, Angela stayed on for perhaps twenty minutes.

It was touching to see them sitting before the saint in such a way. I rejoined my friends Cathy and Eleanor who were standing on my front porch, and the three of us gazed at the three of them gazing at St. Francis.

For the rest of that summer, if I reprimanded young Alice for some behavior, or rather lack of behavior, she would go into the garden and hide behind the little statue of St. Francis, or brush up against it (which, of course, embarrassed me horribly, which was most likely her intent). Angela often was seen seated before the gentle saint, sometimes for no reason that I knew, at other times in response to an event or coming event. For instance, the day I almost adopted a stray kitten that had wandered into the garden. Angela watched me holding the cute little stranger and wasted no time in telling the saint her woes. Seeing Angela praying so intently before the saint, I decided to find the kitten another home.

In fact, the day the priest came by to bless the statue, Angela was sitting in front of it. "You see what I mean," I said to the priest. He stood there for a few minutes, the cat unmoving as well. The priest quietly said, "I see what you mean," and then proceeded to bless Angela and the statue of St. Francis holding a bird with the slender deer at his side. Up until this time, the animals in my life had found their spiritual path without my help – in fact, they had shown me their need for spirituality, their natural devotion and love for the Divine. From this point on I began to consciously teach them, and not just the animals I knew, but every one I came across.

THE CAT WHO WOULD
ONLY FOLLOW BUDDHA

Paula and the Buddha

By this time I was speaking inwardly to every dog and cat I met about God. One afternoon a cat approached me on the corner of Buffalo and Aurora Streets and I began the prayer I used at that time: "Hello little cat. Be a good little cat. Tell Jesus and Mary that you love them. Call on St. Francis when you need him. If you do this, you will go to a beautiful realm one day, where there are trees and gardens and waterfalls, where there is nothing but Love and Happiness. Little cat, pray for yourself and your master or mistress, and for your friends and relatives."

Generally when I gave this prayer, at the mention of Jesus or St. Francis the animal would alertly look around in all directions, as though He Himself or some saint or perhaps angels, some Divinity had come to greet them. In addition, the animal's aura would clear and become bright. Even if the dog or cat were across the street this would happen. I would inwardly teach a dog to pray, and the dog would be looking in all directions within seconds.

In this cat's case, none of these things happened. We stood on the corner of Buffalo and Aurora looking at each other. The cat looked petulant and its aura was rather muddy. I repeated my speech and added a few more things. Nothing.

Not used to failure and a bit exasperated, it was becoming a chilly day in more ways than one. I told the cat that she was hurting Christ's feelings. Moreover, she lived only a block from the Catholic Church so she should be more devout because of this proximity and fortunate exposure; in fact, Mary's statue was visible from where we stood and I pointed to the Church. The cat was unmoved. I pondered awhile. The cat was still standing there, waiting for me to say something she could agree with, which was a good sign. In the end, she had listened and she hadn't run off.

For some reason, and I don't remember why, I began talking to the cat about the Buddha. The cat immediately turned to Light. I continued. I told her to be a good little cat, to be kind to others, and to pray to the Buddha each day. I also suggested that she meditate on "The Mind of Clear Light." She then came up to me and brushed against my legs, and I gave her a pat. How she had come to know and love the Buddha I don't know. But that was definitely her path, there was no mistake about it.

THE LITTLE FIR TREE

The little fir tree sadly stood across the street from the Catholic Church, and just around the corner from me. I believe it was the first tree I taught to pray, and the initial reason for this was that the little fir tree needed tremendous amounts of healing.

It stood by a rental apartment, and no one had taken care of it. Having no water during the hot Ithaca summers, it was terribly stunted and misshapen, and was missing limbs; instead of its natural emerald colour, it looked more or less patched together by shades of brown and dull green – it sported a ragged appearance in general: disease and neglect had taken its toll. This is what I saw on close examination. At first, passing it one evening, in the stillness of the night, I was struck by the beauty of its, well, soul. Even as a child I saw the soul of trees, the light being within the tree. This tree had terrible health, but its soul was gentle and pure. My interest in the tree, at first, was to heal it. As I passed it each day, I prayed and sent it healing, and within months many branches had greened out and its overall form had improved – but the past damage was so great that I actually, and for the first time, enlisted the patient's help. I taught it to pray. Since the little tree stood across from the Catholic Church, in fact, in summer the tree could hear Mass and the choir singing and its upmost branches could even see into the open Church windows, a fact I had reminded the tree of that previous summer, I decided

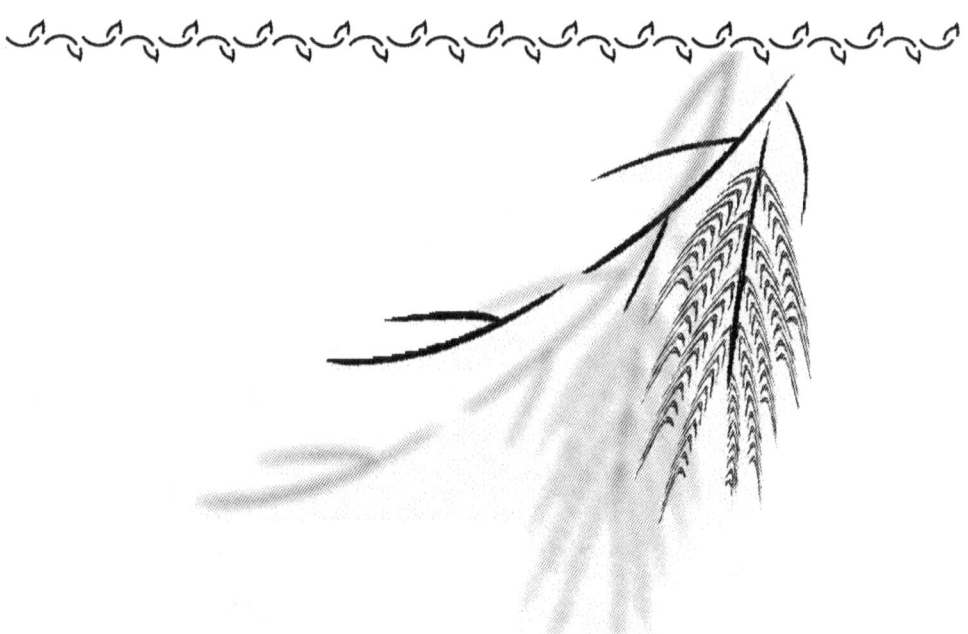

to teach it the Ave Maria. Under the chanting of the moon we slowly intoned the Ave Maria, the night still and clear around us. We did this each night. I asked that the little tree regain its health and that all the missing needles and branches be restored. I reminded the tree, and all the other trees in the neighborhood, that trees had more time to meditate and pray than people. And that the world truly needed prayer, now more than ever before, perhaps more than in the history of the world.

Since I passed the little tree each day, sometimes more than once a day, we had an ongoing relationship, centered on our gentle love and prayers to Mary. One night, for some reason I don't remember, perhaps out of pure affection, I put my hand on one of the tree's needle covered branches. The needles were so brittle that I actually hurt my hand on them. I inwardly said "Ouch" and drew my hand away. I explained the differences between fir tree needles and human hands to the tree and tried again. This time the needles were as soft as the snow that covered them that night.

DOMINIQUE AND THE TREE

At one point, while living on Buffalo Street, I decided to purchase a tree for the garden, for a bit of shade. It would be my first tree, the first tree I had ever chosen and planted, and to care for a living being in this way, be given a piece of life – seemed like such a gift. I had envisioned a delicate flowering cherry tree, but since my decision came out of season, there were none to be had. The man at the nursery managed to talk me into a flowering crabapple tree that was not yet my height and had grown perhaps one leaf. Basically it was a stick almost my height. I decided to call the tree Eleanor, after my friend Eleanor who lived across the garden. I brought Eleanor home and placed her more or less in the middle of the brittle, baked, sparse August lawn. It was a sorry sight, something akin to visions of

Purgatory as described by various saints. At this moment Dominique wafted down the porch steps and into the garden. This in itself was unusual, for she rarely strayed from her L.L. Bean bed. She studied the future tree for a few seconds and then began joyfully barking and running around the tree (and joy was not an emotion Dominique often expressed), around and around and around the tree until I began laughing. At last she laid down beside it, next to the rootball wrapped in burlap, the stick and the leaf above. It was quite a sight.

Who Dominique saw in the tree I do not know. Even I could not discern the soul of the tree until it had leafed out. This happened once with Guinivere and a new shrub as well.

We humans know so little of these interactions between creatures other than ourselves.

My dream is that one day, perhaps while I am walking on this planet we call earth, all the animals and flowers and trees and minerals, insects and reptiles, all the creatures of earth will pray, pray in the way humans were meant to pray. From the Heart, from Love, and continually. This is my dream, that they will pray from their Love of the Divine, and that they will pray for themselves and each other and then the people of the earth and then all the beings and creatures in other realms. Clairvoyantly I can even see this, what such a thing would look like. I see it as many little Hearts of Love and Light joining into one Big Heart or expanse of Light, and within that Greater Heart is contained all the beings and creatures of Earth and all other realms, transparent and bright. This is my vision. May it happen, and may it happen now.

THE PANSIES THAT SANG

Perhaps it started when I was a child, I don't remember how it began. But for years I had sat and waited in fields and meadows hoping to hear the flowers sing. They never did. Or at least I never heard them.

While living in the little house on Buffalo Street, I decided to buy some pansies to put at the feet of the wild rose. The greenhouse was filled with expectant pansy heads, row after row of them – it was difficult to choose between them. Now I always ask, "Who wants to come home with me, to a wonderful garden?"

But at that time I knew not of such dialogue between humans and flowers. So, from the three peat packs of pansies I had chosen, I decided on two – and put the other one back in the far corner of the greenhouse with the other pansies. Outside the greenhouse, a very strange feeling came over me. I couldn't really explain it, but I somehow felt that the tray of blue pansies back in the greenhouse were calling me – and they wanted to come home with me. After some hesitation, I went back and got them.

Once home again, I put the tray of blue pansies at the feet of the wild rose and the other pansies went to other corners of the garden. I thought no more about it save to say "hello" as I walked past, and of course, to water them.

Late in the summer, sitting on my front porch and thinking about various things such as the light in the garden and the clipped topiary maple that looked a bit like an Alice in Wonderland kind of tree–

without warning, and far from my thoughts – I heard flowers sing, a small choir somewhere in the garden. I heard them not exactly with my physical ears, it's hard to explain – more with my mental ears, yet outside me, as though the choir was singing in another realm and yet somehow I could hear them. It was a light, transparent sound, and I could almost see their song, in various colors, as well as I could hear it. It wasn't like the Clap I heard when Nell was hit by the car, nor like the voice calling my name near the Church. Those were true sounds. This was not that. None-the-less it was a small choir, a very gentle choir, a very unearthly and beautiful arrangement of sounds floating across from that corner of the garden where the blue pansies were. It was definitely them. It was the only time I heard them sing.

The following year there were clusters of blue pansies all over the garden, children of the ones that sang. Winters in Ithaca reach temperatures of forty below zero or more – pansies do not ordinarily re-seed themselves. Another interesting thing – the great grandchildren of the pansies that sang bloomed all one winter. My friend Louise and I drove up to my little cottage, a blizzard all around us and we could see them blooming in the snow, along the path. Louise said "What's that" and I said "They're pansies in bloom. They're the great grandchildren of the ones that sang." We got out of the car and went over to them. Louise entered the garden, and as she walked into the wind and tossing gusts of white all around us, gently brushed away some snow with her boot ---yes, blue pansies were blooming all along the brick path, covered in snow.

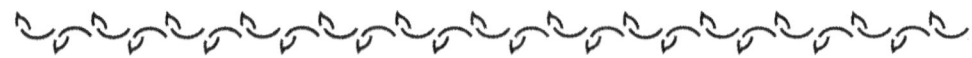

THE LITTLE CAT THAT DIED

The little cat that died was only a week or so old, and he belonged to my friend Dorothy. Dorothy called one late winter night and asked me to come over and see her new little kitten, Bruno. He was very sick, and she sounded very worried. I don't remember how she got him, but Dorothy was always adopting stray cats in the neighborhood. Perhaps he had just wandered in.

I could see at first sight that Bruno would not survive through the night. He was just a baby, a few inches long, and very very ill. He was laboring to even breathe. Dorothy had placed him on a thin and worn, pale blue cotton blanket, and as I looked at Bruno it seemed as though he was as thin and pale as that well worn blanket even though he was new life but a few days old. My heart went out to the little one, and I very gently and carefully lifted him – and as I held him in my hands I could feel that life was already almost gone from the little body.

I asked that he be given all the healing allowed him, and then asked that Bruno be filled and surrounded by the Divine. That was all I could do. Since then I have learned much – to also teach the little one to pray, to send St. Francis or Jesus or Mary to him, or angels to help him transition to other realms ...but the essential prayer was there, to surround and fill him with the Divine energy that some call God, or the Holy Spirit, or whatever other name one wishes to call it.

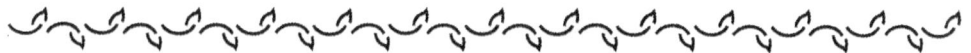

Dorothy saw me to the door, and I asked her to keep in touch about Bruno's condition. The little one was leaving, but I thought it best not to mention that, so I left a few more other words and went home.

A few hours later, I was working on metronome markings for a new score I was writing when a young boy – more like a sprite – appeared to me from another realm. He smiled at me, a big grin, and then performed a little dance for me. Then he vanished.

After some thought – for the event was a bit unexpected and puzzling, even for me – I realized that the "sprite" was, in fact, Dorothy's little kitten Bruno. His brief visit with me from another realm was an innocent and novel way of communicating that he was fine and happy; possibly, he also wished to thank me for my help. The next day Dorothy called to tell me that the kitten had, in fact, "died" the night before.

Why the little kitten appeared to me as a young boy, a sprite-like boy, I do not know. Once I heard the voice of a sad, young man come from the inner being of my little dog Dominique, and the very high voice of a baby from my cat Figaro. These things are mysteries to me, I do not understand them. I also once heard a carrot scream in a blender – but these things were not heard with the physical ears, more with the mental ears, as though coming from or existing in another realm entirely. I can only report what I have experienced, with the poor words I can or cannot find to describe them.

POCO

Poco the dog belonged to my friends who live in Washington D.C. Poco, at a certain point in life, became terrified of the Washington thunderstorms, and often my friends would call me on the phone and ask me to calm their dog. The first time I talked with Poco over the phone my friend said, "What did you say to him? He was a terrified mess and he just laid down and closed his eyes and is taking a nap." In our brief "conversation" I had assured Poco that his mother and father would protect him always. Then I spoke to him of Christ and St. Francis, and told him to be a good dog. I also asked that Poco be given the healing that he needed, and asked Christ to watch over him.

This went on for several months, and finally I suggested that Poco needed a strong spiritual structure, like that of the Catholic Church. In other words, I wanted to raise him Catholic. My friend was a Jew, but she did reluctantly agree to put a little plastic statue of St. Francis by Poco's water dish. My friend said the statue helped.

A year or two later my friends from Washington D.C. came to visit me in Ithaca, and they brought Poco with them. Poco had never been to my house in Ithaca, and he was known to be a confirmed cat chaser as well. As my friend and Poco came up the main path into

the garden, all my cats scattered, and in the confusion my friend failed in her attempt to put the dog's leash on – he got away from her and ran directly to Christ's statue, which was a bit off the garden path, and licked His face. And stood there wagging his tail. My friend and I converged at Christ's statue from our different corners of the garden, and joined Poco who appeared to be the happiest dog on the planet. I was more than a bit amazed because I had never sent Poco a picture of Christ, only the little plastic statue of St. Francis. Either I had sent him mental images of Our Lord without realizing it, or Christ had actually appeared to him. My friend was in shock for many reasons. She was wordless for quite a while and then said, "I never would have believed this if I hadn't seen it with my own eyes."

FIGARO'S MIRACLE

Dominique and Figaro

Figaro is Alice the cat's son. I named him Figaro because he has a remarkable physical resemblance to the cat Figaro in Disney's film Pinocchio. He has a similar temperament as well.

Figaro, from the time he first opened his eyes, thought Dominique was his mother. When Dominique died, he sat in the rocker in the living room and barely moved. For weeks. Luckily, he also always thought that I was his other parent. Since Dominique left for other realms he has rarely left my side except to sit on the picnic table

66

during the summer, where he can effortlessly watch me work in the garden. In the winter he lies next to me on the couch, or stretches out on pillows by the coal stove a few feet away from me. He sleeps next to me at night, either on his back or on his side, with his head on the pillow next to mine, and often he is under the covers with me. It's a huge relationship, and bluntly put, he's the apple of my eye.

We were still renting on Buffalo Street when Figaro was hit by a car. He was hiding under the front porch when I came home from the television studio, and it took quite a bit of time to coax him out. I was not pleased with what I saw. There was much damage – blood, his jaw was hanging from his face, he obviously had a fractured skull and his eyes were already very swollen and bulging out of his head. He looked worse than Nell had.

I called a veterinarian friend and described his condition over the phone. She said she'd be right over. Meanwhile I gently carried him into my downstairs bedroom, and put him on the bed. We prayed, from the heart, and immediately. I asked Christ to heal my little Figaro. I also added hands-on healing for his head and jaw, and spoke to him inwardly, and Figaro began to relax. I mentally sent him everything I could think of, including homeopathic remedies. What was most touching, was that Figaro not only welcomed and trusted the healing I was sending him, he actually seemed to expect it. If I could read his little mind it might sound something like this: He had been hit by a car, he was very injured, and therefore I would have to heal him and he hoped that I would do it quickly.

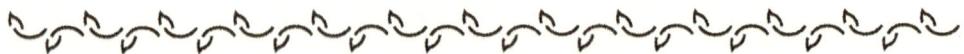

My friend arrived soon after, took one look at him and said "He needs to go to the clinic right now." By this time in life I had seen enough miracles to know one could easily happen – but my friend insisted that Figaro go to the animal hospital immediately, and I did not want to take chances with Figaro's life. Once the correct physical solution is offered, it is often best to take it, for God Himself might have sent it. "All right," I answered. "Just give me some time with him first." She agreed to wait five or ten minutes. Figaro and I prayed to Mary together, and then we took him to the hospital. When I returned home I continued asking for and sending healing. By the time the x-rays were developed there were no fractures – his skull and his jaw were fine. They kept him two nights and then called me the third day. They were watching him – his head was fine, but he wasn't eating. He had lost three pounds and they were worried. I said, "He's not sick, he's not eating because he wants to come home." My friend the veterinarian brought him home and he ate an entire can of Purina cat food the moment he walked in the door. She said, "I should have believed you. We shouldn't have taken him to the clinic." And she insisted on paying all the bills, which amounted to some hundreds of dollars.

These miracles are not the end-all of prayer. The daily devotion is more important. But miracles can win devotees. After this incident, whenever I say an Ave Maria, Figaro comes over and lies beside me, even if his little head was in his crunchies bowl when I began the prayer. Sometimes he puts his hand on my heart while I am praying to Our Lady. He is entirely devoted to Her, and this is the true miracle.

FIGARO AND ST. ANTHONY

Shortly after my grandmother's death, my mother sent me a small statue of Saint Anthony holding the Infant Jesus that had stood on my grandmother's dresser for as long as I could remember. I suspect that I inherited my clairvoyance from my grandmother, for she used to stand before this small statue and say that St. Anthony's expression changed from day to day – some days he smiled at her, and other days he looked sad. My grandmother was an artist, she did needle-point drawings in bold, brilliant colors. She also told many stories of her life in France ...how the children ran into the basement as the bombs fell, and ate jams and jellies while their parents stayed in bed on the second floor, too wearied by war to disturb another night's sleep ...her younger sister Marguerite who played piano for the silent movies, who ran onto their balcony and sang La Marseillaise full voice as the German troops entered Strasbourg ...how her dear, beau-tiful mother and older sister had died taking care of the French sol-diers in the nearby woods ...historic, truthful tales that enchanted me

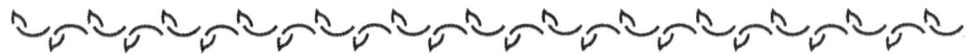

endlessly, so different from my life on earth ....and she would teach me songs in French and German, which we would sing everywhere, even walking down the street. Near the end of her life she had a favorite tree that she would sometimes talk to on her daily walks. She said that she just had this feeling that the tree understood what she was saying. This all made perfect sense to me.

In any case, when I opened the package and took St. Anthony out of his travelling case, Figaro single mindedly came into the kitchen and climbed into my lap. He sat there gazing at the statue, and then very slowly and very very very gently put his paw on St. Anthony's heart. He left it there for quite some time and then looked at the statue for a few more moments, jumped down and went back to whatever he had been doing.

I open packages often, I receive all sorts of presents and scores and catalogue orders in the mail. Figaro was used to such things, I made no new noise or unusual motions with St. Anthony's package; the string was cut with scissors and the tape was cut with the same knife I always used to open boxes. No, Figaro was drawn by what was in the package, before he could even see the contents, for he was in another room.

When I meditate or pray, often Figaro puts his paw on my heart. How would he know where St. Anthony's heart was – I doubt by sight, non-clairvoyant sight. No, he put his hand where he always does, where the Love is emanating from. Even I cannot pinpoint where the Love, the Divine Presence is located in a statue. I feel the Divine Presence, the Divine Love as it enters and surrounds me, but I cannot see it coming from any particular place in the statue. Yet little Figaro, who can't even open his can of Purina cat food can.

70

THE MOSQUITOES
ON BUFFALO STREET

Insects, for me, are more elusive, more inscrutable, more oblique and perhaps more difficult to train than domestic animals. They are also harder to know as individuals, partly because there are so many of them, and partly —well, save differences in posture and dimension, I'm embarrassed to say, insects of a certain species all look alike to me. Except a notable few. And to converse with an insect, or to heal an insect – it helps, at least at first, if you can see them as an individual. The mosquitoes on Buffalo Street were a leap of faith, although I learned much.

For some reason, my last summer on Buffalo Street there were more mosquitoes than usual. In my house. Whereas in other years an occasional mosquito might intrude, his foreboding little whine piercing the silence of the night, that last summer they were so numerous they actually lined up on the walls near the kitchen light.

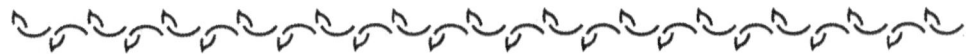

One night I saw them all standing there on the wall and I said to myself, "Do something." As I looked at them I noticed that they were different sizes. Some appeared very young, fragile. Lined up on the wall, near the stained glass lamp I had made in New York City, they looked suddenly ...so innocent. After all, I was the one ready to strike, they were just standing on the wall, maybe even sleeping. I thought, "Why not give them a chance?" Then I thought, "But they all look so alike, how will you know which mosquitoes you've talked to?"

Which was a rational question. My prayer went something like this: "Hello little mosquitoes. I'm perfectly willing to share my home with you. However, it hurts me when you bite me. You can stay here, unharmed, if you don't bite me or the cats. And since I can't tell you apart, you'll have to tell all your friends and relatives and neighbors too, or I'll be forced to kill all of you. And I don't want to kill you." For good measure, I sent them a mental image of the destruction they were facing.

I didn't have another mosquito bite the entire summer. They lined up on the walls, in the light of my stained glass lamp, and slept. Mornings they went outside to return only at night, when the lamps were on. Not a bite.

THE DOG WHO WOULDN'T BEHAVE

A friend, a gentle woman with much inner Light, had more or less lived a contemplative, solitary life. Her home was deep in the country, on an isolated, lonely road, and she was advised to get a dog for protection. After some hesitation – for she worked in town, the dog would be alone long hours, the expense, the commitment and so on – my friend agreed. She located a young, promising German Shepherd and brought him home.

A year or so later we met on a street corner, as often happens in a small town. My friend seemed agitated, almost distraught, and conversation quickly led to her dog. The Dog That Wouldn't Behave was solid protection, he was now fully grown and powerful – but he frightened her. Perhaps because she was gone each day, and came home late many nights after classes or dinners in town, the dog had not been trained properly. Or they had not enough time together to build a relationship. She looked tired and anxious. Should she give him away? What should she do? The Dog Who Wouldn't Behave had snapped and almost bitten her more than once. What if he came at her throat when she was asleep, she asked. Also he didn't listen to her. She was afraid to even take him off his chain, to take him inside the house. In short, she couldn't control him, and she dreaded going home each night.

It sounded like a nightmare. I told her that I would mentally speak to her dog, and that she should let me know what happened, because sometimes animals, as well as humans, needed more than one lecture.

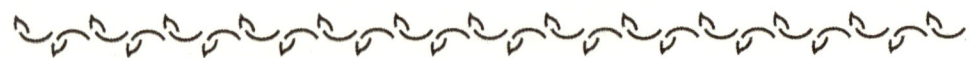

My friend knew that I was clairvoyant, but my having a chat with her would-be-murderer German Shepherd tested her imagination. Being the person she was, she said thank you, and we went off in separate directions.

At that time in my life my teacher Anthony Damiani had mandated that I not use my clairvoyance in this way, except for healing or some other emergency – for I was at that stage where clairvoyance could stay on the psychic, occult level, or it could rise to a Higher level. I felt that my friend's situation, and the dog's future merited its use. So on the way home to teach a piano student, as I walked down the street, I mentally tried to contact the Dog Who Wouldn't Behave.

Within a few seconds, I found him. I saw him outside his house, on a chain, there were trees nearby. He was very clear in my Mind's eye, so I began speaking to him. He was restless at first, not listening at all. So I said something stronger. It went something like this: "Hello big strong dog. I am a friend of your Mistress, and I'm worried about her. You are making her life sad and difficult, and you should be giving her love and protection. That is why she brought you home to live with her – so that you would love each other and care for each other and protect each other." The dog was aware of my presence, but he was not yet convinced that what I was saying was important. He was still pulling on his chain and mostly looking away. I continued: "You must listen to me. Your owner will give you away if you do not change." He began to listen. "Dogs must honor and obey and love their masters. This is a law of the universe. You are making my friend very sad. You should love and protect her" and I more or less continued in this way, in a gentle but firm tone of voice. Finally, after several repetitions and variations the dog sat down and listened, and

I could see that he was thinking. I gave him a few simple prayers to say, and then said good bye.

I never met The Dog That Wouldn't Behave in person, in the body. However, my friend said that my lecture changed his attitude towards life and towards her, and their relationship completely transformed. Her life began to revolve around The Dog That Learned To Behave, and he became her most important and most loving relationship. Many years later when The Dog That Learned To Behave died, my friend was inconsolable.

FIGARO SENDS
LITTLE ALICE HEALING

Alice

Figaro and Alice the cat have always had a difficult relationship. I am
not a psychoanalyst, so I will leave the intricacies and the dynamics
of their relationship to those better trained in the workings of the
emotions and mind. Somebody started the trouble, and someone per-
petuates the problems, but I'm not sure who. All I know is that once
Figaro arrived the family structure fell apart. Since that time I have
felt like a single parent of several small children of different needs and
imbalances – facing chaos day in and day out. In short, the family has
hardly had a peaceful moment since he joined.

This one particular night, Alice was ill. She was so sick that she huddled next to me on the rug. This was actually a very trusting and/or brave thing, because Figaro was in my lap above her and she was well within striking distance. Figaro was, in fact, ready to give her a good swipe – his eyes had that glassy, fixed look and he was switching his expressive tail. Alice perhaps trusted Providence and/or me to protect her, or she was too sick to notice.

Seeing the inevitable outcome – yet also knowing the love Figaro's heart held, I appealed to this higher, more spiritual side. I inwardly told him that Alice wasn't feeling well and needed healing. I had to say this several times, and in several different ways. His tail stopped wagging and he began to relax, his body became its usual limp self and I could see he was listening to me. Then he did a surprising thing. He very slowly and carefully extended his left paw and gently put it on Alice's head. And kept it there, as though he were sending her healing by laying on hands, as I so often had done to him when he was injured or sick. His attention seemed clearly on what he was doing, and it truly appeared as though he was giving her all the Love and Healing he could muster. I was extremely pleased and proud of him, and I told him so, and he left his hand there for quite some time, until Alice felt better and walked away. Whether Figaro healed her, or my prayers healed her or both, we'll never know. But Figaro gave Alice his Heart for those minutes, and in the end that is the essence of all Divine healing.

WASPS I HAVE KNOWN

Wasps have always swarmed to my gardens, perhaps because of the coneflowers and other wildflowers, maybe just because my gardens are so vast and varied. In any case, there were always more wasps walking and drifting along the path than people. I was concerned for my little piano students, but no one was stung so I called a truce with the wasps, and even though their auras left something to be desired, let them be.

However, one day I put my hand on the garden gate, and one of these small tenants stung me. My hand swelled terribly, and stayed swollen – for weeks. Their presence was now a danger to me, perhaps a serious one.

I asked them to please leave. No response. Personally, I did not want to spray toxic chemicals, for all our sakes. In addition, I did not want to be the Hitler of the sullen wasp world, and told them that they were putting me in a terrible position. There was still no response, wasps were everywhere. In fact, the few wasps that boldly drank from the garden hose as I watered looked more annoyed and angry than ever, their auras a terrible tawny brown color. Perhaps they were depressed, I thought. The wasp drinking water on the stone path looked, in a way, innocent enough, he was just drinking water, a life need. He wasn't attacking me, he was just drinking water from the garden hose. That I was on the other end of the hose was an impersonal, external circumstance.

The impasse continued. Finally I told them that if they didn't leave my garden I would be forced to exterminate them. As with the

mosquitoes, there were so many wasps, I never knew who I was speaking to. A friend came over one day and said: "Talk to their leader." I immediately told the wasp nearest to me to give a message to their leader: Leave my garden or be killed. That was my final offer. There was no response, although that little wasp did fly off into the distance as though delivering my message.

Days went by, and I watched them come and go. They even seemed more respectful. Some came very close to me and made it clear they had no interest in harming me, in fact some were almost deferential, polite. It seemed that they were trying to communicate. This was hopeful, but not the solution. Politeness was not my goal. However, this gave me an idea. I decided to explain my side in detail. There was an uncomfortable looking potential emissary, a wet, bedraggled little wasp by my feet. His aura was pitiful. This is what I said: "Hello, little wasp. I can see that you don't want to hurt me. I have an important message for your Leader. I could die if you sting me. And a human life is very, very valuable in the eyes of God. And I have many little students coming through the garden every day. You could harm them too, even if you don't mean to. Even though you don't want to hurt me, or my friends, accidents can happen. We could step on you by accident. And then we might die. Tell your leader that you can be in the garden every morning, the garden is yours. But when I wake up and come into the garden you all must leave. Or I will be forced to kill you, to protect myself and my friends. Go tell your leader, little wasp." And the wasp flew off into the distance.

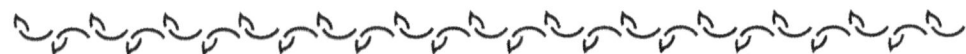

The next day, when I went into the garden –there were no wasps. I was amazed. Yes, there were one or two stragglers, and I shooed them off, reminding them of our arrangement. Since I stayed up all night, they had the garden until almost noon, which seemed fair to me. Occasionally there was an afternoon wasp that I would allow to drink from the garden hose, but even those I spoke to about accidents and they would listen and then leave. The garden was free of danger at last. Each new spring we would renew our pact, and it was a friendly one, their auras were clear and bright when we spoke. It was a happy arrangement and the best solution for everyone involved.

A few years later we moved to Lincoln Street. Here I have an even larger garden, and a grape arbor which attracted every wasp in the neighborhood and perhaps beyond. We moved in during August, and wasps were everywhere. And in this case they felt that they owned the property; legally this might have been true. However, I cornered a little wasp drinking from a puddle of water on the path and spoke to him as I had to my friends on Buffalo Street. I had to send messages to their leader more than once, but they did finally agree to a morning/afternoon agreement. There were a few insurgents, until one afternoon I rescued a drowning wasp very gently and with much love from a garden bucket that had filled with rain water. I told him that accidents could happen, not only to me but also to them as he had just discovered. I then sent him healing and taught him to pray, and told him to teach everyone he met. He flew off and I have barely seen another wasp since.

80

ANGELA AND THE
INFANT OF PRAGUE

A few years ago, I ordered a most beautiful statue of the Infant of Prague, that is of the Infant Jesus. When He came out of His box His aura looked a little blue, and I wondered if He had suffered a difficult trip in the mail. Perhaps for this reason, I occasionally carry Him around the downstairs rooms, showing Him the paintings and icons of His Mother and the other saints and angels. Also, being the Child Jesus, I sometimes asked myself if He might not be a bit lonely alone on His shelf – although I did put a small wooden train beside Him there.

In any case, our first tour of the downstairs was a few years ago, towards dawn. I said nothing aloud, nor made any unusual noise–

81

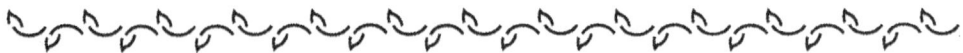

yet my eldest cat Angela immediately came running down the stairs. She sleeps on the guest bed upstairs all night, on the wedgewood blue thermal cotton blanket. She plunged downstairs and towards me, brushing against my legs and almost tripping me as I took the Infant of Prague around the house, until I began to laugh. She began meowing, and looked up at me pitifully, and when I reached the kitchen with the Divine Infant in my arms, she actually stood on a chair, her forefeet on the back of the chair, trying to get near the Infant Jesus. Standing there crying and pleading, she looked at the statue and then at me and then at the statue until finally I let her rub up against Him, the Little Lord of the Universe. She began to purr, and stayed with us until He was safely back on His shelf, next to the wooden train.

That Angela begged to touch the Infant did not seem unusual. Figaro had done the same with St. Anthony, Angela and Alice often brushed up against St. Francis in the garden – what puzzles me even now: how did Angela know I had taken the Infant of Prague off His shelf? Was there a burst of energy that she felt even from her bed in the middle room upstairs, or do the animals have a constant communion with these Divine Beings and saints, like a radar connection, so that they know if a painting or statue is moved? Or was it even something else – did she read my mind, or did angels tell her to run down the stairs, or perhaps even the Infant of Prague Himself?

These things we will never know.

ANGELA AND CHIDVALASANANDA

For years, from when I first became a television producer, I had wanted to produce a television show on the spiritual life of animals – the narration would be easy, but I had no photos or video footage for visuals. And the events related in this book could not easily be duplicated. If I took a studio camera on the street, and videotaped the reactions of animals to prayer or statues, surely people would think I had put some scent on the statue to attract them, or that the reactions onscreen were due to someone waving or calling the animals off camera. I didn't know what to do, so I did nothing, and eventually I realized there would never be a television show if I waited for the perfect solution.

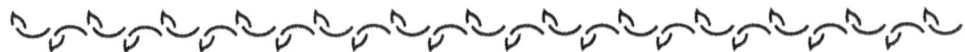

Therefore, after a late production session at the studio, I signed out a 460 camera, a tripod and lights and brought them home. I would ask Figaro, Alice and Angela to pray and let the camera run. It would not be spectacular to watch, but at least I could give a narrative account of my experiences, and the animals watching would benefit even if the humans remained skeptical. This was my reasoning, for better or for worse. So I brought the studio camera and lights and tripod home, and told my cats the next day that I was making a television show for other cats and dogs to watch on the topic of prayer. I then urged them to pray very hard on camera, for the sake of all the animals watching. I said this for two reasons (1) Alice absolutely hates being on camera, and the only other footage I have of her for television is her tail as she runs from the room (2) Cats can be a bit stubborn, and often when you want them to do one thing they do the opposite. And I truly wanted them to pray on camera as an example for the cats and dogs and other animals who might watch the show.

While filming, I inwardly asked my cats to ignore the bright camera lights, the camera and tripod and just pray. And they did. Even with tempting outside summer noises to investigate. Figaro spent some of his prayer time facing the garden and listening to the birds and thinking about his spot on the picnic table and very much wanting to go outside – however, he did stay on the table and pray none the less. I was very proud of all of them, especially Alice. Alice, who absolutely detests cameras of all kinds, especially video cameras, prayed for twenty minutes straight – even while Franz, who was off camera, loudly ate crunchies in the bowl three feet away from her. Still I felt that the television show needed at least one big, visible reaction to a picture or statue in order to be believable to the average human.

The problem is that cats do not like to show emotion, they prefer to act nonchalant or worse. Therefore, the visible reactions generally take place the first time they meet a statue or picture – and my cats have known all our paintings and statues for years. Discouraged, I looked around the room – and there was a photograph of Chidvalasananda that Angela would not be too familiar with – it was hidden behind some other things on the wooden box in the living room. Angela was praying on camera, facing the camera, on the arm of the living room sofa, eyes closed. I quietly put the photograph of Chidvalas against the back of the couch, a bit to Angela's right and behind her. I went back behind the camera to watch. Angela did, in fact, feel the energy coming from the photograph – she half opened her eyes and turned her head in the direction of the photograph. She probably thought the energy came from someone she knew, because when she saw Chidvalasananda's face she literally did a double take. On camera. Then she turned, very slowly, sideways on the arm of the sofa, towards Chidvalas, so that her back end was neither facing the camera nor Chidvalasananda. And she then closed her eyes and continued praying. Luckily, I have that on film also.

FIGARO AND THE UPRIGHT PIANO

When Mariette and I moved to Lincoln Street, she brought her mahogany upright piano. Large and heavy, with carved scrollwork, it was a nice contribution to the house. We put it against a wall in the living room, thinking it would work nicely as a second piano for concertos.

There were already two Steinway grand pianos in the house. There were also two grand pianos in the studio out back, because my friends have a habit of leaving their grand pianos with me when they leave town. So in all, there were three Steinway grand pianos, a Chickering grand – and Mariette's upright piano. Needless to say, the upright was never played, it more or less sat in the corner of the living room holding up photographs of various sages and saints and vases of flowers.

One evening after dinner, Mariette and I were relaxing on the living room couch, reading the New York Times. Figaro, who weighs eighteen pounds and is tall enough to turn doorknobs while standing with his back feet on the floor, strode purposely towards the upright piano, stood on his back feet and placed his front paws on the wood strip of the keyboard. We watched him with interest. First of all, he had never gone to the upright before, and secondly he looked ridiculous standing there, swaybacked, his little belly hanging in front – and yet his head was erect and he was looking at the keyboard as though he were about ready to play something. After a grand pause, Figaro raised his right arm very high, in a Rubinstein arm position, and dropped it unhesitatingly, his paw landing impeccably on one note. The note was beautifully articulated, a gorgeous rich tone, and he held it for quite a long time, listened to it ring solidly through the room and then fade, dropped back to the floor and found his food dish in the kitchen. "That was amazing," I said. "What a sound." "Why did he do it?" asked Mariette, and after some thought I said, "He's never seen or heard an upright piano. He wanted to know what kind of sound it made." It must be true, because Figaro only played that one note on that one evening – he has never played the upright again, not in all the years since.

THE PLANTS ON LINCOLN
STREET PRAY FOR FRANZ

Franz was a sleek, handsome black cat with white feet and long
whiskers. He moved in with us on Buffalo Street one summer
evening many years ago. At that time he was close to death, and went
directly to the hospital for testing. It was obvious that he hadn't had
a home in a long while, if ever, and the first six months with us were
basically spent curled up on my bed. He was wise and calm, a true
peacemaker, and for his non-aggression he was rewarded with many
scars given to him by the neighborhood bully cat who has since
reformed.

It became clear that Franz had never been held by a human being. He
froze in the air, his legs stiffened and groped for the ground, his body
tense and breathless – in short, Franz was horrified by the height and
motion. As time went on this changed somewhat, but never completely.

One night he was sick, and I took him over to the bay tree and the
coleus and other plants which tier the south window of the kitchen.
This was not an unusual tour, we often had said hello to the plants in
the south window, but this particular night Franz only wished to put
his feet on terra firma. He was, in fact, ignoring the coleus who was
spilling over her pot in such a graceful and abundant way, the bay tree
with a few new buds, the jasmines and orange tree, the geraniums
and other plants even though his nose was almost in the amaryllis.
He was struggling to get down. I stepped back a foot or two to put
him down, and on the way said, "Little plants, pray for Franz, he is

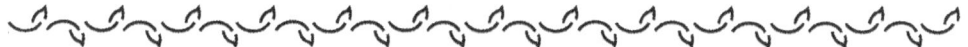

very sick tonight." As I did so Franz stopped struggling. In fact he froze – not from fear, but as though he were paying deep attention to something that had just begun. He lifted his head, the rest of his frail body hanging from my arms; Franz seemed fully alert yet motionless, his ears forward – he was staring ahead and facing the plants. Franz appeared to be in a trance. His aura brightened and the plants were shining with light – they were sending Franz prayers and love, I could both see it and feel it. So could Franz. He remained motionless in that position for so many minutes that I became restless and finally put him down.

Because of this incident I learned that plants as well as animals and people need to be reminded to pray. I say this because I had asked them to pray for Franz only days earlier and apparently they had forgotten. Franz and I can tell you that if all the creatures of earth would put aside their own private, self-absorbed thoughts and would instead immerse themselves in the Divine and radiate that Love – the veil to the Kingdom of God would be parted. It would literally be Heaven on Earth.

ANGELA GETS TRAPPED

Angela

Angela, the Queen, my beautiful and fluffy longhaired cat Angela. Angela, the mother of so many beautiful children, Angela who took care of kittens that were not even her own children, but strays and friends and neighbors. Angela whose heart is so strong I can feel her heart's love a room away... a block away....

Angela was missing for days, and we began to worry the first night because Angela never missed meals. Never. She was gone for four days and I clairvoyantly began to try to find her. I saw her in a building, but the picture was fuzzy around the edges, I couldn't quite see where she was. She was trapped, but she was doing fine; and she was nearby.

At first I thought she might be in the abandoned shed next door. I went over and called for her – no answer. The shed was locked and had no windows. There was no way she could have gotten in, but we called the owners and checked inside. No Angela. All we could do was wait and hope that wherever she was, someone would free her.

What worried us most was that we were experiencing a terrible heat wave, and if Angela was without water she might die. Every day I asked about her, and she was fine. However, on the seventh day I got that she was in trouble. I said to Mariette, "We have to find Angela. She's in trouble." And she was. She might not survive more than another day.

We combed the neighborhood, blocks in every direction – but my Heart kept bringing me back to our block, and up the street. It was as though every time we walked in the wrong direction, a Love left me, a force left me, and I knew that I was heading the wrong way.

In the end, we did find her – we miraculously spotted her through the window of an abandoned house up the street, two houses past the empty shed we had examined days earlier. Had we known that the house was unoccupied, we would have looked there sooner. We did-n't know. That Angela was in the window at that moment – could only be Providence, or Angela's heart finding ours. For if she hadn't come to the window at that moment – we would never have found her.

As it turned out, she was taking care of an abandoned kitten that had wandered into the house. The owner, not knowing they were there, had locked them in. Angela was severely dehydrated, and it took her some time to recover, but otherwise she was fine. The little baby cat she was taking care of died in the house. She brought us to him when

we found her, as though she trusted us to bring him back to life. In fact, we could barely convince her to leave him behind. This is the depth of her heart.

When I said that I clairvoyantly tried to find Angela – I don't usually try to use my clairvoyance in this way. As I said earlier, the true clairvoyance, clairvoyance at its highest, is seeing the Divine everywhere. And I do. The kind of clairvoyance I used to find Angela is on a lower level – the more physical/emotional level, the psychic level. I use this generally only for healing purposes, or to find someone, either in this realm or another realm.

For me, clairvoyance, or direct perception, proves that time and space do not truly exist. If one can clairvoyantly see the future, or know what is happening across the globe – then what are time and space? There is no time and space, and clairvoyants are living proof of this. It is all happening in the Heart, the spiritual Heart, where the individual soul meets the Divine Mind's impressions, i.e. our world and the events and people that we perceive. We perceive them outside ourselves – and conventionally, in conventional reality, this is true – but in Ultimate Reality or Truth, no. All that we experience, perceive, first happens in the Heart, or soul. And ultimately, clairvoyants are standing there, directly perceiving events in the Heart or Head, depending on what level they are operating from. Some clairvoyants can stand in either place, others not. The clairvoyance is not the main thing – no, it is the Love, the Higher Love, the Divine Love that one finds in the Heart, or soul – that is the end all of all spirituality, whether one happens to be clairvoyant or not. And that is how I actually found Angela – by our hearts, our Love. Love, the Divine Love brought me to her whereas my pictorial clairvoyance – could not.

CHIP TEACHES FIGARO
HOW TO CLIMB THE GRAPE ARBOR

I call all the squirrels in our yard Chip, in memory of Chip the First. Chip the First came to a sad end, and was buried in the front garden. As a tribute to the immortality of the soul, and also because I have a bit of trouble recognizing one squirrel from another – all squirrels found in the garden are named Chip.

Chip the First taught Figaro how to climb the grape arbor.

Let me explain. Figaro, as I have already mentioned in previous stories, is a male cat and very large. He is also very clumsy. On Buffalo Street I always left the bathroom window open for the cats; Angela and Alice would effortlessly leap from the window to the rim of the bathtub and then daintily onto the floor. No problem. Figaro, as a baby, would watch them do this. One day I heard a crash in the bathtub. It was Figaro. Another day I heard a crash in the bathtub. It was Figaro. From then on I also left the kitchen window open, which even I could get through easily.

When we moved to Lincoln Street, Angela and Alice found a way

93

onto the grape arbor within days. They jumped to the studio roof, and then easily walked onto the arbor. Figaro watched them do this for three years. To make matters worse, birds made a nest directly over his favorite spot on the picnic table. He watched them come and go above his head, listened to their conversations endlessly, heard them learn to sing, and more or less suffered a constant humiliation. I did see him once try to climb the metal poles that hold up the grape arbor. He ran towards the pole, leapt into the air, almost missed the pole but somehow grabbed on, the weight of his body swung him around the pole, feet in the air, until he finally let go and fell to the ground. It was hard for a parent to watch. From that point on he sat on the picnic table, under the birds and more or less pretended they didn't exist.

About this time Chip the First began climbing the grape arbor. He chose an easy route, up and down a sturdy grape vine that ran at a forty-five or so degree angle up from the ground to the arbor. Chip the First's path to the arbor was directly across the stone path from Figaro's favorite spot on the picnic table.

Figaro watched him the entire summer, from the safety of the picnic table. One thing I know about Figaro, he is not a fast thinker, but he ponders. He thinks things over for a very long time before he acts, but ultimately he acts.

One day, late summer, I was sweeping the path under the arbor when bits of leaves and grapes and twigs began falling all around me. I looked up and saw a big shadow through the grape leaves, meowing. It was Figaro. He had taken Chip's route up the grape arbor. I had to get a ladder to retrieve him. By the following fall he did learn to come down the same way he got up.

94

FIGARO'S DEPARTURE
FOR OTHER REALMS

Little Figaro departed our planet after fifteen good years on earth, towards the end of the summer of 2001. He left bravely, with Faith and Hope. But not until an Experience in the garden.

Figaro was diagnosed with a form of cancer , and I was not allowed to interfere. As his breathing became more labored, he became more depressed. Not knowing what to do, I became more depressed as well.

One day I decided to join him in the garden and pray. I sat down next to Figaro on the wooden bench under the crabapple tree, and looked at the statue of Jesus and the Sacred Heart under the lilacs. I began to pray to Christ. Then I prayed to Our Lady, asking that Figaro be taken care of and comforted in his distress. I opened my eyes to pat Figaro, and he had turned to face the statue of Our Lady by the topiary fir tree. His eyes were closed and his little head bowed.

I gave a sigh. He was still pretty desolate.

I closed my eyes again and this time I prayed to St. Francis. Again I asked that Figaro be taken care of and comforted in his distress.

Suddenly I had a vision – St. Francis was running, running very quickly away and upwards. And under his right arm, held like a football player holds a football when running down the field towards the goal – was a small bundle of Light. When I looked more closely

at that small bundle of Light, I could distinguish the form and features of little Figaro. Then the vision vanished.

Figaro saw the vision as well.

I say this because his entire being had changed. For the better. He was a changed boy, and he happily jumped down and went over to his favorite spot in the garden. When Mariette came home than evening after work she commented: Figaro isn't depressed anymore, what happened?

From this I gathered that his depression stemmed from not knowing his future – Figaro was a slow thinker, but a thinker nonetheless. Knowing he was going to leave us, he was worried because he didn't know what was going to happen to him.

He was peaceful and strong, and pretty much his old self to the end.

FIGARO'S LAST GIFT

Figaro gave me a big Gift before he left. This happened out in the garden, on a mild summer night on the back porch stoop.

Well, I was sitting on the back stoop, he was a bit to my right on his favorite spot on the picnic table to the right of the stoop, under a vine. I went outside to join him that night, he spent most of his time out in the garden that last week.

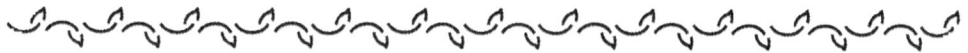

It was a beautiful night, gently warm with a little breeze. I was enjoying the quiet and the company of my little friend Figaro when suddenly the tranquility of the garden was harshly broken by the loud clanking of bottles and cans. I was annoyed. Every night our neighbor did this, how in the world could two people accumulate so many cans each day, break the peaceful atmosphere, etcetera – and then I looked at little Figaro. He had lifted his head and was intently, very intently listening. I imagined him saying to himself, "Oh, there is our wonderful neighbor, dear Jim." He listened until all the sounds had stopped and our neighbor's kitchen door closed.

Then an ant rounded the top rim of the picnic table and headed towards Figaro. Figaro watched him with deep interest. A leaf moved – he watched that as well. In fact, nothing was uninteresting or mundane or ignored – Figaro treated every event in his small world on the picnic table with total reverence and interest. As I sat there I realized that Figaro, who was laboring for breath with every inhale, was taking every second that was left to him and expanding it into days or weeks or years of Experience. And I also realized that each of us could do that, live many happy lifetimes in one, if we wished. That every moment of life was Precious and Sacred, that every second of every Life could be this way if we wished it.

And I have to say – that since that summer night with Figaro, I happily anticipate the sound of the clanking cans and bottles from next door; the clanking sounds now have a magical, musical ring. The musical, magical ring of Life.

DIVINE HEALING & MIRACLES

The Divine Healing techniques taught to me by my teacher are outlined in the preceding stories. These are the techniques that I use and they have never failed me. One merely asks for what is needed and then trusts that the request has been heard and answered. Then one says thank you.

However, as I have already mentioned in those stories, we are not allowed to interfere with the Divine Plan, the Will of God. We trust that God knows what is best for a being's soul, and that He Loves us all more than we could ever imagine. Therefore we say thank you and trust the outcome, whether we are given a visible miracle or not.

If you truly love your animal or plant, then you are already sharing in the Divinity around us – for there, in our Love, we most easily meet the Divine. If the Love is great enough a simple "God help us please" can bring about a miracle, as in Guinivere's story. Or enough Ave Marias as in the story about little Nell the cat. There is no one prescription in Divine Healing, there are thousands, millions of ways to talk to God – for each heart is different. You will find your own way, you only need to begin.

In short, the basis of all prayer and healing, the overriding and most important thing is L O V E May all the creatures and kingdoms of Earth find the Divine Love, find the Golden Arrow.

EPILOGUE

That animals learn from each other shouldn't
surprise us – but somehow it does. My young friend
Niel was visiting and one day said: My mom doesn't
think animals have souls. I replied, "Well they do, and
I can think of some cats and dogs that will get to Heaven
before I do." We humans know so little of the interactions
all around us, we miss the Beauty and the Love and the intri-
cacy that is everywhere. The qualities of intelligence, compassion, communication, emotions, ethics, growth, spirituality, to
name but a few... are not solely human. They are given to and
found in every species – and it seems that other creatures
respect these qualities in each other, even if we do not.
Sometimes I look into the garden, and all the connections that
exist there – between the grass and the worms and the bugs and
the squirrels and the cats and the trees and the flowers and the
soil and the leaves and the stems and the air and the rain – a
myriad of connections and communications that humans
walk through with so little reverence or even awareness.

Tonight my prayer is to thank the Divine for the diversi-
ty of our universe and all the beings and creatures that
inhabit it. That Divinity can manifest in such myriad
ways is beyond human comprehension and is, in itself,
a testimony to the Infinite Nature of God.

May all beings one day know this Love & Gratitude
for all that we have been given here on Earth.

Peace to all that read these lines.

THE GOLDEN ARROW

—a prayer given to St. Faustina of Poland—

May The most Sacred, The most Holy,
The most Adorable, The most Unutterable
and Mysterious Name of God
be forever praised, blessed,
loved, adored and glorified
in Heaven and on the Earth
and under the Earth
by all the creatures of God....

Figaro

Figaro under the grape arbor

Anyone with stories or photos for a Volume II of
The Spiritual Life of Animals and Plants
please send to the author at:
405 E. Lincoln Street
Ithaca, New York 14850
(include a stamped, self-addressed envelope for the return of your materials)
•
for all other correspondence email
dominique_press@hotmail.com

www.ingramcontent.com/pod-product-compliance
Lightning Source LLC
Chambersburg PA
CBHW030348290526
45785CB00004B/1656